AQA Science Chemistry

Revision Guide

New GCSE

D0177043

John Scottow

Series Editor
Lawrie Ryan

Nelson Thornes

AQA examination questions are reproduced by permission of the Assessment and Qualifications Alliance.

Published in 2011 by:
Nelson Thornes Ltd
Delta Place
27 Bath Road
CHELTENHAM
GL53 7TH
United Kingdom

11 12 13 14 15 / 10 9 8 7 6 5 4 3 2 1

A catalogue record for this book is available from the British Library

ISBN 978 1 4085 0831 2

Cover photograph: John Feingersh/Blend Images/Corbis

Page make-up by Wearset Ltd, Boldon, Tyne and Wear

Printed and bound in Spain by GraphyCems

Photo acknowledgements
Page 1 Martyn F. Chillmaid.

Unit 1
C1.2.3 iStockphoto; C1.2.4 AKP Photos/Alamy; C1.3.1 Fotolia; C1.3.2 Fotolia; C1.3.3 iStockphoto; C1.3.4 Chris R Sharp/Science Photo Library; C1.3.5 iStockphoto; C1.3.6a iStockphoto; C1.3.6b Eco Images/Universal Images Group/Getty Images; C1.4.1 iStockphoto; C1.4.4 Photolibrary; C1.4.5 Fotolia; C1.5.1 Paul Rapson/Science Photo Library; C1.5.2 Fotolia; C1.5.3a iStockphoto; C1.5.3b CC Studio/Science Photo Library; C1.6.3 iStockphoto; C1.6.4 Fotolia; C1.7.3 Stocktrek RF/Getty Images.

Unit 2
C2.2.5a Alamy/Rob Walls; C2.2.5b Innershadows/Fotolia; C2.2.6 Pasieka/Science Photo Library; C2.3.3 Bloomberg/Getty Images; C2.3.6 Sciencephotos/Alamy; C2.4.9a Martyn F. Chillmaid; C2.4.9b Fuse/Getty Images.

Unit 3
C3.1.1a CCI Archives/Science Photo Library; C3.1.1b Science Photo Library; C3.1.4 Tony Craddock/Science Photo Library; C3.1.5 Andrew Lambert Photography/Science Photo Library; C3.2.1a Martyn F. Chillmaid/Science Photo Library; C3.2.1b iStockphoto; C3.2.2 Pink Sun Media/Alamy; C3.2.3 iStockphoto; C3.3.5a Dane Andrew/Corbisnews; C3.3.5b Toby Melville/Reuters/Corbis; C3.4.1 David Taylor/Science Photo Library; C3.4.2a Charles D. Winters/Science Photo Library; C3.4.2b Science Photo Library; C3.4.3 Andrew Lambert Photography/Science Photo Library; C3.4.5a Patrick Dumas/Eurelios/Science Photo Library; C3.4.5b Patrick Landmann/Science Photo Library; C3.5.2 Anyka/iStockphoto; C3.5.3 Lawrence Migdale/Science Photo Library; C3.5.4 Michael Hilgert/Agefotostock/Photolibrary.

Chemistry   Contents

Welcome to AQA GCSE Chemistry!

Key points

At the start of each topic are the important points that you must remember.

Maths skills

This feature highlights the maths skills that you will need for your Science exams with short, visual explanations.

This book has been written for you by the people who will be marking your exams, very experienced teachers and subject experts. It covers everything you need to revise for your exams and is packed full of features to help you achieve the very best that you can.

Key words are highlighted in the text and are shown **like this**. You can look them up in the glossary at the back of the book if you're not sure what they mean.

Where you see this icon, you will know that this topic involves How Science Works – a really important part of your GCSE.

These questions check that you understand what you're learning as you go along. The answers are all at the back of the book.

Many diagrams are as important for you to learn as the text, so make sure you revise them carefully.

Anything in the Higher boxes must be learned by those sitting the Higher Tier exam. If you're sitting the Foundation Tier, these boxes can be missed out.

The same is true for any other places that are marked [**H**].

AQA Examiner's tip

AQA Examiner's tips are hints from the examiners who will mark your exams, giving you important advice on things to remember and what to watch out for.

Bump up your grade

How you can improve your grade – this feature shows you where additional marks can be gained.

At the end of each chapter you will find:

End of chapter questions

These questions will test you on what you have learned throughout the whole chapter, helping you to work out what you have understood and where you need to go back and revise.

And at the end of each unit you will find:

AQA Examination-style questions

These questions are examples of the types of questions you will answer in your actual GCSE, so you can get lots of practice during your course.

You can find answers to the End of chapter and AQA Examination-style questions at the back of the book.

1.1 Atoms, elements and compounds

- There are about 100 different **elements** from which all substances are made. The periodic table is a list of the elements.

▶ 1 What substances are shown in the periodic table?

- Each element is made of one type of **atom**.
- Atoms are represented by chemical symbols, e.g. Na for an atom of sodium, O for an atom of oxygen.
- The elements in the periodic table are arranged in columns, called **groups**. The elements in a group usually have similar properties.

▶ 2 What atom does H represent?

- Atoms have a tiny **nucleus** surrounded by **electrons**.
- When elements react, their atoms join with atoms of other elements. **Compounds** are formed when two or more elements combine together.

▶ 3 What type of substance is sodium chloride, NaCl?

AQA Examiner's tip

Remember that a symbol represents one atom of an element.

Key words: element, atom, group, nucleus, electron, compound

Key points

- All substances are made of atoms.
- Elements are made of only one type of atom.
- Chemical symbols are used to represent atoms.
- Compounds contain more than one element.

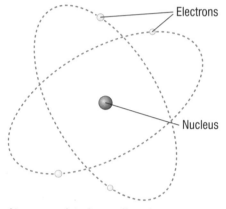

Electrons

Nucleus

Atoms consist of a small nucleus surrounded by electrons

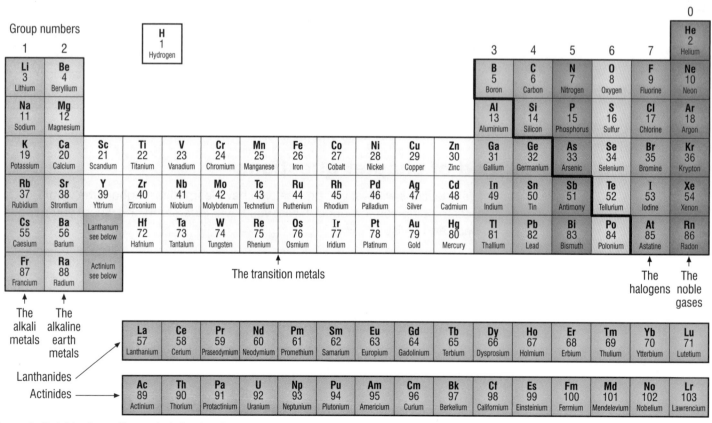

The periodic table shows the symbols for the elements

1.2 Atomic structure

- The nucleus at the centre of an atom contains two types of particle, called **protons** and **neutrons**. Protons have a positive charge and neutrons have no charge.

- Electrons are tiny negatively charged particles that move around the nucleus. An atom has no overall charge. That is because the number of protons is equal to the number of electrons and their charges are equal and opposite (proton +1 and electron –1).

▶ **1** *Why are atoms neutral?*

- All atoms of an element contain the same number of protons. This number is called the **atomic number** (or proton number) of the element. Elements are arranged in order of their atomic numbers in the periodic table. The atomic number is also the number of electrons in an atom of the element.

- The **mass number** is the total number of particles in the nucleus of an atom, so it is the number of protons plus the number of neutrons.

▶ **2** *How many protons, neutrons and electrons are there in an atom of aluminium (atomic number 13, mass number 27)?*

Key points

- The nucleus of an atom is made of protons and neutrons.

- Protons have a positive charge, electrons a negative charge and neutrons are not charged.

- The atomic number (or proton number) of an element is equal to the number of protons in the nucleus of its atoms.

- Elements are arranged in order of their atomic numbers in the periodic table.

- The mass number is the sum of the protons and neutrons in the nucleus of an atom.

> **Maths skills**
>
> Work out the number of each type of particle in an atom of fluorine from its atomic number of 9 and its mass number of 19.
> Number of protons = atomic number = 9
> Number of electrons = number of protons = 9
> Number of neutrons = mass number – atomic number = 19 – 9 = 10

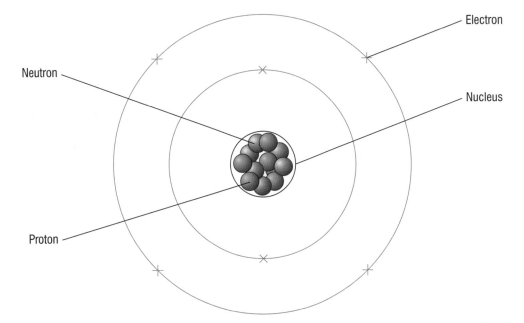

Understanding the structure of an atom gives us important clues to the way substances react together

Key words: proton, neutron, atomic number, mass number

1.3 The arrangement of electrons in atoms

Key points

- The atoms of the unreactive noble gases (in Group 0) all have very stable arrangements of electrons.

- Electrons in atoms are in energy levels that can be represented by shells.

- Electrons in the lowest energy level are in the shell closest to the nucleus.

- Electrons occupy the lowest energy levels first.

- All the elements in the same group of the periodic table have the same number of electrons in their highest energy level (outer shell).

- Each electron in an atom is in an **energy level**. Energy levels can be represented as **shells**, with electrons in the lowest energy level closest to the nucleus.

- The lowest energy level or first shell can hold two electrons, and the second energy level can hold eight. Electrons occupy the lowest possible energy levels. The **electronic structure** of neon with 10 electrons is 2,8. Sodium with 11 electrons has the electronic structure 2,8,1.

⟹ **1** *Draw a diagram to show the electronic structure of an atom of aluminium (atomic number 13).*

- Elements in the same group of the periodic table have the same number of electrons in their highest energy level, e.g Group 1 elements have one electron in their highest energy level.

⟹ **2** *Explain why nitrogen and phosphorus are both in Group 5 in the periodic table.*

- Group 1 elements include lithium, sodium and potassium. These elements react quickly with water and with oxygen.

- The atoms of the unreactive noble gases (in Group 0) all have very stable arrangements of electrons.

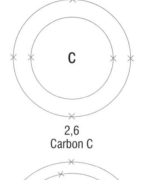

2,6
Carbon C

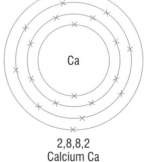

2,8,8,2
Calcium Ca

We can draw shells as circles on a diagram, with electrons represented by dots or crosses

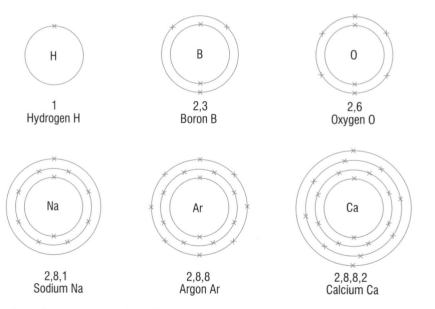

1
Hydrogen H

2,3
Boron B

2,6
Oxygen O

2,8,1
Sodium Na

2,8,8
Argon Ar

2,8,8,2
Calcium Ca

Once you know the pattern, you should be able to draw the energy levels of the electrons in any of the first 20 atoms (given their atomic number)

Bump up your grade

You should be able to work out the numbers of protons, neutrons and electrons for any atom from its atomic number and mass number.

Key words: energy level, shell, electronic structure

1.4 Forming bonds

Key points

- Compounds of metals bonded to non-metals have ionic bonds.

- The formula of an ionic compound shows the simplest ratio of ions.

- Compounds of non-metals have covalent bonds.

- The formula of a molecule shows the number of atoms in the molecule.

AQA Examiner's tip

The formula for ionic compounds and metallic elements is the simplest possible ratio, such as $MgCl_2$ or $NaCl$.

AQA Examiner's tip

For substances made of molecules the formula shows the number of atoms in the molecule, such as O_2 or C_2H_6.

- When different elements combine they form compounds.

- When a metal reacts with a non-metal, ions are formed. Metal atoms lose one or more electrons to form positively charged ions. Non-metal atoms gain electrons to form negatively charged ions. The oppositely charged ions attract each other strongly and the compound has **ionic bonds**.

1   Name an example of a compound with ionic bonds.

- The chemical formula of an ionic compound tells us the simplest ratio of ions in the compound. For example, NaCl shows that sodium chloride is made from equal numbers of sodium ions and chloride ions.

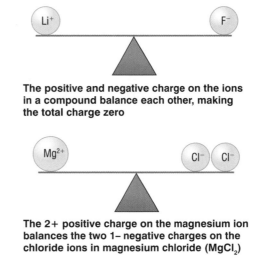

The positive and negative charge on the ions in a compound balance each other, making the total charge zero

The 2+ positive charge on the magnesium ion balances the two 1– negative charges on the chloride ions in magnesium chloride ($MgCl_2$)

2   Calcium chloride has the formula $CaCl_2$. What does this tell you about the compound?

- When non-metals combine, their atoms share electrons to form **covalent bonds** and molecules are formed.

- The chemical formula of a molecule tells us the number of atoms that have bonded together in the molecule. For example, H_2O shows that a water molecule contains two hydrogen atoms and one oxygen atom. Covalent bonds can be shown as lines between the atoms that are bonded together.

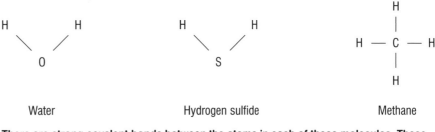

Water   Hydrogen sulfide   Methane

There are strong covalent bonds between the atoms in each of these molecules. These are shown as lines between the symbols of the atoms in the molecule.

3   The formula of propane is C_3H_8. What does this tell you about propane?

Key words: ionic bond, covalent bond

1.5 Chemical equations

Student Book
pages 32–33 **C1**

Key points

- Atoms get re-arranged in chemical reactions.

- The mass of the products is equal to the mass of reactants.

- Symbol equations should always be balanced.

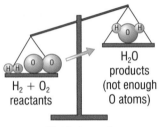

Not balanced

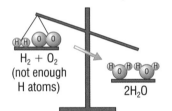

Still not balanced!

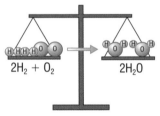

Balanced at last!

Making an equation balance

AQA Examiner's tip

Remember that in a balanced symbol equation a large number multiplies all of the atoms in the formula that follows.

- In chemical reactions the atoms in the reactants re-arrange themselves to form new substances, the products.

- Atoms are neither created nor destroyed in a chemical reaction. So the number and type of atoms remains the same before and after the reaction.

- This means that the mass of the **products** equals the mass of **reactants**.

- It also means that we can write chemical equations to represent reactions.

- Word equations only give the names of the reactants and products. Symbol equations show the numbers and types of atoms in the reactants and products.

- When symbol equations are written they should always be balanced.

- This means that the numbers of each type of atom should be the same on both sides of a symbol equation.

> **1** *Explain as fully as you can what this balanced symbol equation tells you:* $Mg + 2HCl \rightarrow MgCl_2 + H_2$

Making an equation balance

Symbol equations are balanced by changing the large numbers in front of the formulae of the reactants and products.

You should balance equations by changing only the large numbers. Never change the small (subscript) numbers because this changes the formula of the substance.

> **2** *Balance these equations:* **a** $H_2 + Cl_2 \rightarrow HCl$
> **b** $Na + O_2 \rightarrow Na_2O$
> **c** $Na_2CO_3 + HCl \rightarrow NaCl + H_2O + CO_2$

Bump up your grade

To improve your grade when taking the Higher Tier paper, learn how to balance a symbol equation given the formulae of the reactants and products.

Maths skills

In the formulae in symbol equations, small (subscript) numbers multiply only the atom they follow.

For example: In H_2SO_4 we have H_2 = 2 atoms of hydrogen, S = one atom of sulfur, O_4 = 4 atoms of oxygen.

If more than one atom within a formula has to be multiplied, brackets are used.

$Mg(NO_3)_2$ (one magnesium ion and two nitrate ions) is made from

one atom of magnesium 1×2 atoms of nitrogen 3×2 = 6 atoms of oxygen.

Large numbers multiply all atoms in the formula that follows. So $2CO_2$ (two molecules of carbon dioxide) shows a total of two carbon atoms and four oxygen atoms.

Key words: product, reactant

1 Sort these substances into elements and compounds:
Ca, CH_4, H_2, HCl, MgO, Ne, O_2, SO_2.

2 What are the names and numbers of the particles in an atom of sodium (atomic number 11, mass number 23)?

3 What determines the order of the elements in the periodic table?

4 Draw a diagram to show the electronic structure of sulfur (atomic number 16).

5 Explain why boron and aluminium are both in the same group in the periodic table.

6 Name the type of bonds in each of these compounds:
CaO, C_2H_6, H_2O, KCl, LiCl, $MgCl_2$, NH_3, Na_2O, PCl_3.

7 Explain what happens to the atoms when a sodium atom reacts with a chlorine atom.

8 The equation for a reaction of lead nitrate is:
$Pb(NO_3)_2 + 2KI \rightarrow 2KNO_3 + PbI_2$

a Write a word equation for this reaction.

b Give the name and number of each type of atom in the products.

9 Calcium carbonate decomposes when heated to produce calcium oxide and carbon dioxide. 20.0 g of calcium carbonate produced 11.2 g of calcium oxide. What mass of carbon dioxide would be produced?

10 Balance these symbol equations: [H]

a $Ca + O_2 \rightarrow CaO$

b $Na + H_2O \rightarrow NaOH + H_2$

c $CH_4 + O_2 \rightarrow CO_2 + H_2O$

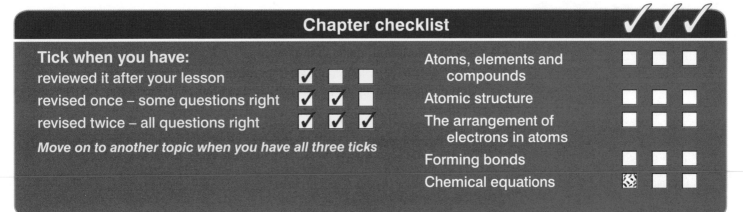

Chapter checklist ✓ ✓ ✓

Tick when you have:				Atoms, elements and compounds	□ □ □
reviewed it after your lesson	✓	□	□		
revised once – some questions right	✓	✓	□	Atomic structure	□ □ □
revised twice – all questions right	✓	✓	✓	The arrangement of electrons in atoms	□ □ □
Move on to another topic when you have all three ticks				Forming bonds	□ □ □
				Chemical equations	▨ □ □

Student Book
pages 36–37 **C1**

2.1 Limestone and its uses

Student Book
pages 38–39 **C1**

Key points

- Limestone is made mainly of calcium carbonate.
- Limestone is used as a building material and to make calcium oxide and cement.
- Cement mixed with sand, aggregate and water makes concrete.
- Calcium carbonate decomposes when heated to make calcium oxide and carbon dioxide.

- We quarry large amounts of limestone rock because it has many uses.
- Blocks of limestone can be used for building. Limestone is used to make calcium oxide and **cement**.
- We make **concrete** by mixing cement with sand, aggregate and water.
- Limestone is mainly **calcium carbonate**, $CaCO_3$.
- When heated strongly, calcium carbonate decomposes to make calcium oxide and carbon dioxide. This is done on a large scale in lime kilns. The equation for this reaction is:

$$CaCO_3 \rightarrow CaO + CO_2$$
calcium carbonate   calcium oxide   carbon dioxide

- This type of reaction is called **thermal decomposition**.

▶ **1** *List the ways in which limestone and products made from limestone are used in the building industry.*

AQA Examiner's tip

Thermal decomposition means 'breaking down by heating'. You need to make both points – 'breaking down' and 'by heating' – to get full marks.

Key words: cement, concrete, calcium carbonate, thermal decomposition

2.2 Reactions of carbonates

Key points

- Metal carbonates decompose when heated to produce the metal oxide and carbon dioxide.
- Carbonates react with acids to produce a salt, water and carbon dioxide.
- Carbon dioxide turns limewater cloudy.

- All metal carbonates react in similar ways when heated or when reacted with acids.
- Metal carbonates decompose to the metal oxide and carbon dioxide when they are heated strongly enough.
- A Bunsen burner flame cannot get hot enough to decompose sodium carbonate or potassium carbonate.

▶ **1** *What are the products when zinc carbonate is heated strongly?*

- All carbonates react with acids to produce a salt, water and carbon dioxide gas. Limestone is damaged by acid rain because the calcium carbonate in the limestone reacts with acids in the rain.
- Calcium hydroxide solution is called limewater. **Limewater** is used to test for carbon dioxide. The limewater turns cloudy because it reacts with carbon dioxide to produce insoluble calcium carbonate.

▶ **2** *Write a word equation for the reaction of magnesium carbonate with hydrochloric acid.*

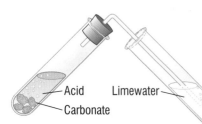

Acid   Limewater

Carbonate

The test for carbonates

Key word: limewater

Student Book
pages 40–41

C1

2.3 The 'limestone reaction cycle'

Student Book
pages 40–41

Key points

- Thermal decomposition of calcium carbonate produces calcium oxide and carbon dioxide.
- Calcium oxide reacts with water to produce calcium hydroxide.
- Calcium hydroxide is an alkali that can be used to neutralise acids.
- Calcium hydroxide reacts with carbon dioxide to produce calcium carbonate.

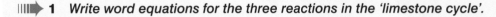

Bump up your grade

If you are taking the Higher Tier paper, you should be able to write balanced symbol equations for the three reactions in the 'limestone cycle'.

St Paul's Cathedral in London is built from limestone blocks

- When heated strongly the calcium carbonate in limestone decomposes to **calcium oxide** and carbon dioxide.
- When water is added to calcium oxide they react to produce **calcium hydroxide**.
- Calcium hydroxide is an alkali and so it can be used to neutralise acids. For example, it is used by farmers to neutralise acidic soils and in industry to neutralise acidic gases.
- Calcium hydroxide is not very soluble in water but dissolves slightly to make limewater.
- Calcium hydroxide reacts with carbon dioxide to produce calcium carbonate, the main compound in limestone.

▐▐▶ **1** *Write word equations for the three reactions in the 'limestone cycle'.*

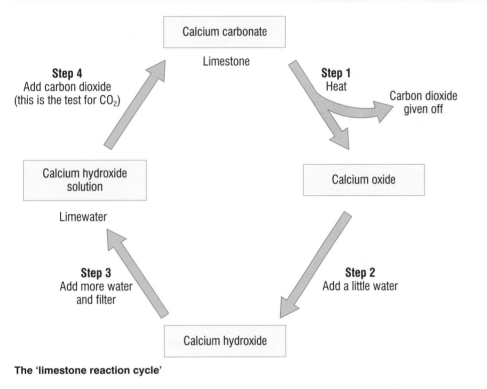

The 'limestone reaction cycle'

Key words: calcium oxide, calcium hydroxide

Student Book
pages 42–43 **C1**

2.4 Cement and concrete

Key points

- Cement is made by heating limestone with clay in a kiln.
- Mortar is made by mixing cement and sand with water.
- Concrete is made by mixing aggregate with cement, sand and water.

Concrete is mixed, poured and left to set

- To make cement, limestone is mixed with clay and heated strongly in a kiln. Theproduct is ground up to make a fine powder.
- Cement is mixed with sand and water to make **mortar**. The mortar is used to hold bricks and blocks together in buildings.
- Concrete is made by adding aggregate to cement, sand and water. Small stones or crushed rock are used as aggregate. The mixture can be poured into moulds before it sets to form a hard solid.

⟫ **1** *What are the differences between cement, mortar and concrete?*

AQA *Examiner's tip*

You should have studied developments in using limestone, cement and concrete but you will not be tested on what you know about these developments in the exam.

Key word: mortar

Student Book
pages 44–45 **C1**

2.5 Limestone issues

Key points

- There are good and bad points about quarrying for limestone.
- Limestone, cement and concrete are needed as building materials.
- Quarrying and processing limestone and its products have negative impacts on the environment.

- We depend on limestone to provide building materials. Cement and concrete are needed in most buildings.
- Quarrying limestone can have negative impacts on the environment and on people living near to the quarries.
- Cement works are often close to limestone quarries. Making cement involves heating limestone with clay in large kilns. This uses a large area of land and a lot of energy.

⟫ **1** *Sort the following into advantages and disadvantages for an area in which limestone is to be quarried.*
   a *More employment opportunities for local people*
   b *Dust and noise*
   c *More traffic*
   d *Loss of habitats for wildlife*
   e *More customers and trade for local businesses*
   f *Improved roads*

AQA *Examiner's tip*

You may be given information in the examination about building materials or the processes needed to make them so that you can consider their positive benefits and the negative aspects of their production and use.

1 Which of these is the formula for the main compound in limestone?
$CaCl_2$, $CaCO_3$, $CaSO_4$, $Ca(OH)_2$

2 How is cement made?

3 Name the four substances used to make concrete.

4 What is meant by 'thermal decomposition' of a compound?

5 Name the products formed when calcium carbonate is heated strongly.

6 Write a word equation for the reaction of calcium oxide with water.

7 Limewater goes cloudy when mixed with carbon dioxide. Explain why, using an equation in your answer.

8 Explain, as fully as you can, why acids damage limestone.

9 Farmers spread calcium hydroxide on fields with acidic soils. Explain why, naming the type of reaction that takes place and the property of calcium hydroxide on which this reaction depends.

10 Balance this symbol equation:
$K_2CO_3 + HCl \rightarrow KCl + H_2O + CO_2$ [H]

Chapter checklist

Tick when you have:
reviewed it after your lesson ☑ ☐ ☐
revised once – some questions right ☑ ☑ ☐
revised twice – all questions right ☑ ☑ ☑
Move on to another topic when you have all three ticks

Limestone and its uses ☐ ☐ ☐
Reactions of carbonates ☐ ☐ ☐
The 'limestone reaction cycle' ☐ ☐ ☐
Cement and concrete ☐ ☐ ☐
Limestone issues ☐ ☐ ☐

Student Book
pages 48–49

C1

3.1 Extracting metals

Key points

- Metals are usually found in the Earth's crust. They are often combined chemically with other elements such as oxygen.
- An ore contains enough metal to make it worth extracting the metal.
- The method we use to extract a metal depends on its reactivity.
- Unreactive metals are found in the Earth as the metal.
- The oxides of metals less reactive than carbon can be reduced using carbon.

- Rock that contains enough of a metal or a metal compound to make it worth extracting the metal is called an **ore**.

- Mining ores often involves digging up large amounts of rock. The ore may need to be concentrated before the metal is extracted. These processes can produce large amounts of waste and may have major impacts on the environment.

▸ **1** *What is an ore?*

- A few unreactive metals, low in the **reactivity series**, such as gold are found in the Earth as the metal. Gold can be separated from rocks by physical methods. However, most metals are found as compounds. So then the metals have to be extracted by chemical reactions.

- Metals can be extracted from compounds by displacement using a more reactive element. Metals which are less reactive than carbon can be extracted from their oxides by heating with carbon. A **reduction** reaction takes place as carbon removes the oxygen from the oxide to produce the metal. This method is used commercially if possible.

▸ **2 a** *Name two metals that have oxides that can be reduced by carbon?*
  b *What do we call the removal of oxygen from a metal oxide?*

Bump up your grade

If you are taking the Higher Tier paper, you should be able to write a balanced symbol equation for the reduction of a named metal oxide by carbon.

Key words: ore, reactivity series, reduction

An open-cast copper mine

Student Book
pages 50–51

C1

3.2 Iron and steels

Key points

- Iron oxide is reduced in a blast furnace to make iron.
- Iron from the blast furnace is too brittle for many uses.
- Most iron is converted into alloys called steels.
- Steels contain carefully controlled quantities of carbon and other elements.

- Many of the ores used to produce iron contain iron(III) oxide. Iron(III) oxide is reduced at high temperatures in a **blast furnace** using carbon. The iron produced contains about 96% iron. The impurities make it hard and brittle and so it has only a few uses as **cast iron**. Removing all of the carbon and other impurities makes pure iron, but this is too soft for many uses.

▸ **1** *Why does iron from the blast furnace have only a few uses?*

- Most iron is used to make **steels**. Steels are **alloys** of iron because they are mixtures of iron with carbon and other elements. Alloys can be made so that they have properties for specific uses.

- The amounts of carbon and other elements are carefully adjusted when making steels. Low-carbon steels are easily shaped and high-carbon steels are hard.
- Some steels, such as **stainless steels,** contain larger quantities of other metals. They resist corrosion.

▶ **2** *Why are steels more useful than pure iron?*

Key words: blast furnace, cast iron, steel, alloy, stainless steel

Steels have many uses in modern buildings

Student Book
pages 52–53   **C1**

3.3 Aluminium and titanium

Key points

- Aluminium and titanium resist corrosion. They also have low densities compared with other strong metals.
- Aluminium and titanium cannot be extracted from their oxides using carbon.
- Aluminium and titanium are expensive because extracting them involves many stages and requires large amounts of energy.

Titanium turbine blades in a jet engine

- **Aluminium** has a low density and, although it is quite high in the reactivity series, it is resistant to corrosion.
- Aluminium is more reactive than carbon and so its oxide cannot be reduced using carbon.
- It has to be extracted by electrolysis of molten aluminium oxide. The process requires high temperatures and a lot of electricity. This makes aluminium expensive to extract.
- Pure aluminium is not very strong, but aluminium alloys are stronger and harder. They have many uses.

▶ **1** *Why is it expensive to extract aluminium from its ore?*

- **Titanium** is resistant to corrosion and is very strong. It also has a low density compared with other strong metals.
- Titanium oxide can be reduced by carbon, but the metal reacts with carbon making it brittle.
- Titanium is extracted from its ore by a process that involves several stages and large amounts of energy. The high costs of the process make titanium expensive.

▶ **2** *Why is titanium a very useful metal for making aircraft engines?*

AQA *Examiner's tip*

You do not need to remember any further details of the methods used to extract these metals.

Bump up your grade

Learn some of the properties and uses for each of the metals named in this chapter.

Key words: aluminium, titanium

3.4 Extracting copper

Key points

- Most copper is extracted from copper-rich ores by smelting.
- Copper can be purified by electrolysis.
- Bioleaching and phytomining are new ways to extract copper from low-grade ores.
- Copper can be obtained from solutions of copper salts by displacement or electrolysis.

- Copper can be extracted from **copper-rich ores** by **smelting**. This means heating the ore strongly in a furnace.

- Smelting produces impure copper, which can be purified by electrolysis.

- Smelting and purifying copper ore require huge amounts of heating and electricity.

- Copper-rich ores are a limited resource. Scientists are developing new ways of extracting copper from low-grade ores. These methods can have less environmental impact than smelting.

- **Phytomining** uses plants to absorb copper compounds from the ground. The plants are burned and produce ash from which copper can be extracted.

- **Bioleaching** uses bacteria to produce solutions containing copper compounds.

> 1 Why are new ways of extracting copper being researched?

- Solutions of copper compounds can be reacted with a metal that is more reactive than copper, such as scrap iron, to **displace** the copper.

- Copper can also be extracted from solutions of copper compounds by electrolysis.

> 2 What three ways can be used to produce copper metal from its compounds?

Pure copper plates produced by electrolysis

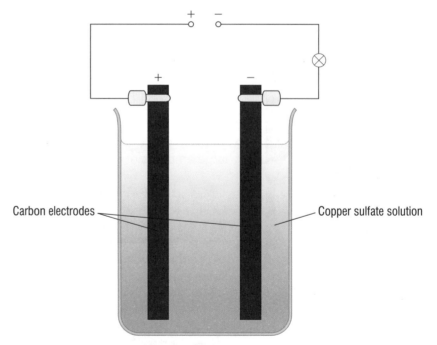

Carbon electrodes — Copper sulfate solution

Extracting copper metal using electricity

Key words: copper-rich ore, smelting, phytomining, bioleaching, displace

3.5 Useful metals

The position of the transition metals in the periodic table

Transition metals

Key points

- The transition metals are found in the central block of the periodic table.
- Transition metals have properties that make them useful for building and making things.
- Most of the metals we use are alloys.

Alloys are used to make some musical instruments

AQA **Examiner's tip**

When asked for the properties of alloys, many students include cost or cheapness but cost is not a property of a substance.

- Elements from the central block of the periodic table are known as the **transition metals**.
- They are all metals and have similar properties.
- They are good conductors of heat and electricity.
- Many of them are strong, but can be bent or hammered into shape. These properties make them useful as materials for buildings, vehicles, containers, pipes and wires.

▌▌▌➡ **1** *What properties make transition metals useful materials for making things?*

- Copper is a very good conductor of heat and does not react with water. It can be bent but it is hard enough to keep its shape. These properties make it useful for making pipes and tanks in water and heating systems. It is a very good conductor of electricity as well and so it is used for electrical wiring.

▌▌▌➡ **2** *What properties are needed for electrical wiring?*

- Most of the metals we use are not pure elements.
- Pure iron, copper, gold and aluminium are soft and easily bent. They are often mixed with other elements to make alloys that are harder so that they keep their shape.
- Iron is made into steels (see C1 3.2).
- Gold used for jewellery is usually an alloy.
- Most of the aluminium used for buildings and aircraft is alloyed.
- Copper alloys include bronze and brass.

▌▌▌➡ **3** *Why is the gold used for wedding rings mixed with other metals?*

Key word: transition metal

3.6 Metallic issues

Key points

- There are social, economic and environmental issues associated with exploiting metal ores.
- Recycling saves energy and limited resources.
- There are drawbacks as well as benefits from the use of metals in structures.

Steel girders are used in many buildings

- Mining for metal ores involves digging up and processing large amounts of rock. This can produce large amounts of waste material and effect large areas of the environment.

- Recycling metals saves the energy needed to extract the metal. Recycling saves resources because less ore needs to be mined. Also, less fossil fuel is needed to provide the energy to extract the metal from its ore.

▐▐▐▶ **1** *Why should we recycle aluminium cans?*

- The benefits of using metals in construction should be carefully considered against the drawbacks. Some examples are shown in the table below.

Some benefits of using metals in construction	Some drawbacks of using metals in construction
<ul><li>they are strong</li><li>they can be bent into shape</li><li>they can be made into flexible wires</li><li>they are good electrical conductors</li></ul>	<ul><li>obtaining metals from ores causes pollution and uses up limited resources</li><li>metals are more expensive than other materials such as concrete</li><li>iron and steel can rust</li></ul>

▐▐▐▶ **2** *Use the information in this chapter to explain the benefits and drawbacks of using steel for girders in buildings.*

AQA Examiner's tip

You do not need to remember details or specific examples of uses of metals beyond those given in C1 Topics 3.1 to 3.5, but you should be prepared to discuss and evaluate information you are given in the examination.

Bump up your grade

To gain the highest grade, you should be able to write a clear evaluation of information you are given about metals, identifying benefits and drawbacks and giving a conclusion.

1 What is the name for rock that is mined from which metal can be extracted economically?

2 Why is gold found in the Earth as the metal?

3 What are the typical properties of 'transition metals'?

4 Explain why most of the metals we use are not pure elements.

5 Describe a reaction that is used to get iron from iron oxide. Write a word equation for the reaction.

6 Name three types of steel and give an important property for each one.

7 Explain why all steels are alloys.

8 Give three properties that make aluminium a useful metal.

9 Give three reasons why titanium is expensive.

10 Suggest three reasons why we should recycle iron and steel.

11 Name two methods, other than smelting, of extracting copper from low-grade ores. Describe how one of these methods can be used to make copper.

12 Balance these equations:
$$Fe_2O_3 + C \rightarrow Fe + CO_2$$
$$Na + TiCl_4 \rightarrow Ti + NaCl$$

[H]

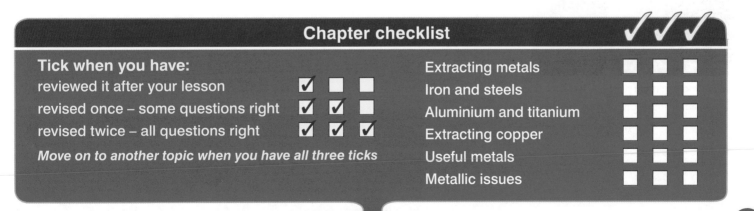

Chapter checklist						
Tick when you have:				Extracting metals		
reviewed it after your lesson	✓	☐	☐	Iron and steels		
revised once – some questions right	✓	✓	☐	Aluminium and titanium		
revised twice – all questions right	✓	✓	✓	Extracting copper		
Move on to another topic when you have all three ticks				Useful metals		
				Metallic issues		

Student Book
pages 62–63

C1

4.1 Fuels from crude oil

Key points

- Crude oil is a mixture of many different compounds.

- Distillation can be used to separate mixtures of liquids.

- Most of the compounds in crude oil are hydrocarbons – they contain only hydrogen and carbon.

- Alkanes are saturated hydrocarbons. They contain as many hydrogen atoms as possible in their molecules.

AQA Examiner's tip

Remember that the boiling point of a substance is the temperature at which its liquid boils when it is heated. When its gas is cooled it condenses at the same temperature.

An oil refinery at night

- Crude oil contains many different compounds that boil at different temperatures. These burn under different conditions and so crude oil needs to be separated to make useful fuels.

- We can separate a **mixture** of liquids by **distillation**. Simple distillation of crude oil can produce liquids that boil within different temperature ranges. These liquids are called **fractions**.

> **1** *What are fractions?*

- Most of the compounds in crude oil are **hydrocarbons**. This means that their molecules contain only hydrogen and carbon. Many of these hydrocarbons are **alkanes**, with the general formula C_nH_{2n+2}. Alkanes contain as many hydrogen atoms as possible in each molecule and so we call them **saturated hydrocarbons**.

> **2** *How can you tell that the substance with the formula C_5H_{12} is an alkane?*

- We can represent molecules in different ways. A molecular formula shows the number of each type of atom in each molecule, e.g. C_2H_6 represents a molecule of ethane. We can also represent molecules by a **displayed formula** that shows how the atoms are bonded together.

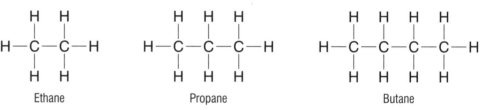

Ethane   Propane   Butane

We can represent alkanes like this, showing all of the atoms and the covalent bonds in each molecule

> **3** *What is the molecular formula of butane?*

Key words: mixture, distillation, fraction, hydrocarbon, alkane, saturated hydrocarbon

4.2 Fractional distillation

AQA **Examiner's tip**

Simple distillation is done in steps by heating the mixture to different temperatures. Fractional distillation is done continuously by vaporising the mixture and condensing the fractions at different temperatures.

- Crude oil is separated into fractions at refineries using **fractional distillation**. This can be done because the boiling point of a hydrocarbon depends on the size of its molecule. The larger the molecule, the higher the boiling point of the hydrocarbon.

- The crude oil is vaporised and fed into a fractionating column. This is a tall tower that is hot at the bottom and gets cooler going up the column.

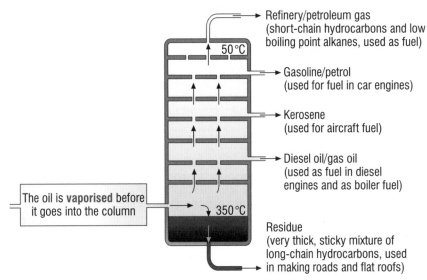

Refinery/petroleum gas
(short-chain hydrocarbons and low boiling point alkanes, used as fuel)

50 °C

Gasoline/petrol
(used for fuel in car engines)

Kerosene
(used for aircraft fuel)

Diesel oil/gas oil
(used as fuel in diesel engines and as boiler fuel)

The oil is **vaporised** before it goes into the column

350 °C

Residue
(very thick, sticky mixture of long-chain hydrocarbons, used in making roads and flat roofs)

We use fractional distillation to separate crude oil into fractions. Each fraction contains compounds with similar boiling points.

- Inside the column there are many trays with holes to allow gases through. The vapours move up the column getting cooler as they go up. The hydrocarbons condense to liquids when they reach the level that is at their boiling point. Different liquids collect on the trays at different levels and there are outlets to collect the fractions.

- Hydrocarbons with the smallest molecules have the lowest boiling points and so are collected at the top of the column. The fractions collected at the bottom of the column contain hydrocarbons with the highest boiling points.

    1 *Why are different hydrocarbons collected at different levels of a fractional distillation column?*

- Fractions with low boiling ranges have low **viscosity** so they are runny liquids. They are very **flammable** so they ignite easily. They also burn with clean flames, producing little smoke. This makes them very useful as fuels.

    2 *What properties would you expect for a fraction that is collected one-third of the way up a fractionating column?*

Key words: fractional distillation, viscosity, flammable

4.3 Burning fuels

- When pure hydrocarbons burn completely they are **oxidised** to carbon dioxide and water. However, the fuels we use are not always burned completely. They may also contain other substances.

1 *Write a word equation for the complete combustion of ethane.*

- In a limited supply of air **incomplete combustion** may produce **carbon monoxide**. Carbon may also be produced and some of the hydrocarbons may not burn. This produces solid particles that contain soot (carbon) and unburnt hydrocarbons called **particulates**.

2 *Name four possible products of the incomplete combustion of a hydrocarbon.*

- Most fossil fuels contain sulfur compounds. When the fuel burns these sulfur compounds produce **sulfur dioxide**. Sulfur dioxide causes acid rain.

- At the high temperatures produced when fuels burn, oxygen and nitrogen in the air may combine to form **nitrogen oxides**. Nitrogen oxides also cause acid rain.

3 *What environmental problem is caused by sulfur dioxide and nitrogen oxides?*

Key words: oxidised, incomplete combustion, carbon monoxide, particulate, sulfur dioxide, nitrogen oxide

Key points

- Burning hydrocarbons in plenty of air produces carbon dioxide and water.
- Burning hydrocarbons in a limited supply of air may produce carbon monoxide and solid particles.
- Any sulfur compounds in the fuel burn to produce sulfur dioxide.
- Oxides of nitrogen can be formed when fuels burn under extreme conditions.

Bump up your grade

If you are taking the Higher Tier paper, you should be able to write balanced symbol equations for the complete and incomplete combustion of a hydrocarbon when given its formula.

4.4 Cleaner fuels

- We burn large amounts of fuels and this releases substances that spread throughout the atmosphere and affect the environment.

- Burning any fuel that contains carbon produces carbon dioxide. Carbon dioxide is a greenhouse gas that many scientists believe is the cause of **global warming**. Incomplete combustion of these fuels produces the poisonous gas carbon monoxide. It can also produce tiny solid particulates that reflect sunlight and so cause **global dimming**.

1 *Name the product of incomplete combustion that scientists believe causes global dimming.*

- Burning fuels also produces sulfur dioxide and nitrogen oxides. These gases dissolve in water droplets and react with oxygen in the air to produce acid rain.

- We can remove harmful substances from waste gases before they are released into the atmosphere. Sulfur dioxide is removed from the waste gases from power stations. Exhaust systems of cars are fitted with catalytic converters to remove carbon monoxide and nitrogen oxides. Filters can remove particulates.

Key points

- Many scientists believe that carbon dioxide from burning fuels causes global warming.
- Sulfur dioxide and nitrogen oxides cause acid rain.
- Particulates cause global dimming.
- Pollutants can be removed from waste gases after the fuel is burned.
- Sulfur can be removed from fuels before they are burned so less sulfur dioxide is given off.

Sulfur can be removed from fuels before they are supplied to users so that less sulfur dioxide is produced when the fuel is burned.

▷ **2** *What two methods are used to reduce the amount of sulfur dioxide produced by burning fuels?*

Key words: global warming, global dimming

A combination of many cars in a small area and the right weather conditions can cause smog to be formed. This is a mixture of **SM**oke and f**OG**.

Student Book
pages 70–71

C1

Key points

- Biodiesel can be made from vegetable oils.
- Biofuels are a renewable source of energy that could be used instead of fossil fuels.
- There are advantages and disadvantages of using biodiesel.
- Ethanol made from sugar is a biofuel.
- Hydrogen is a potential fuel for the future.

AQA *Examiner's tip*

You do not need to remember specific examples of advantages and disadvantages of biodiesel, but should be able to evaluate any information that is given in the examination.

4.5 Alternative fuels

- **Biofuels** are made from plant or animal products and are renewable. **Biodiesel** can be made from vegetable oils extracted from plants.
- There are advantages to using biodiesel. For example, it makes little contribution to carbon dioxide levels. This is because the carbon dioxide given off when it burns was taken from the atmosphere by plants as they grew.
- There are also disadvantages, for example the plants that are grown for biodiesel use large areas of farmland.
- Ethanol made from sugar cane or sugar beet is a biofuel. It is a liquid and so can be stored and distributed like other liquid fuels. It can be mixed with petrol.

▷ **1** *Name two biofuels.*

How Science Works

- Using hydrogen as a fuel has the advantage that it produces only water when it is burned.
- However, it is a gas so it takes up a large volume. That makes it difficult to store in the quantities needed for combustion in engines.
- It can be produced from water by electrolysis but this requires large amounts of energy.

▷ **2** *Give one advantage and one disadvantage of hydrogen as a fuel.*

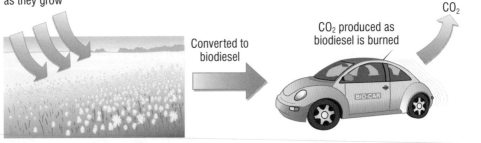

Plants absorb CO_2 as they grow

Converted to biodiesel

CO_2 produced as biodiesel is burned

CO_2

Cars run on biodiesel produce very little CO_2 overall, as CO_2 is absorbed by plants as the fuel is made

Growing plants for biodiesel uses a lot of farmland

Key words: biofuel, biodiesel

1 Why is crude oil separated into fractions?

2 Name the products when ethane, C_2H_6, burns completely.

3 Give three reasons why fractions with lower boiling points are more useful as fuels.

4 Name two fuels that can be made from renewable sources.

5 Some exhaust fumes contain particulates. What are particulates and how are they produced?

6 Explain why burning some fuels produces sulfur dioxide.

7 Propane, C_3H_8, is used as a fuel for cookers. Explain why propane should always be burned in a plentiful supply of air.

8 Why are some scientists concerned about the carbon dioxide produced by burning fossil fuels?

9 Pentane has the formula C_5H_{12}. Draw a displayed formula for pentane and write down four facts about pentane that you can deduce from its formula.

10 Explain what happens in a fractional distillation column used to separate crude oil.

11 Write a balanced symbol equation for the complete combustion of ethanol, C_2H_6O.   [H]

12 Write a balanced symbol equation for the reaction of hydrogen with oxygen. Explain why scientists are interested in using hydrogen as a fuel.   [H]

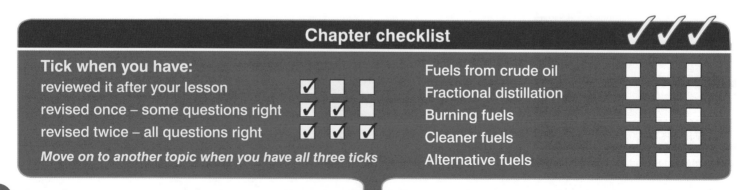

Chapter checklist ✔✔✔

Tick when you have:

reviewed it after your lesson   ✔ ☐ ☐

revised once – some questions right   ✔ ✔ ☐

revised twice – all questions right   ✔ ✔ ✔

Move on to another topic when you have all three ticks

Fuels from crude oil	☐	☐	☐
Fractional distillation	☐	☐	☐
Burning fuels	☐	☐	☐
Cleaner fuels	☐	☐	☐
Alternative fuels	☐	☐	☐

5.1 Cracking hydrocarbons

Key points

- Hydrocarbon molecules can be broken down by heating them with steam to a very high temperature or by passing their vapours over a hot catalyst.

- Cracking produces alkanes and alkenes.

- Alkenes are unsaturated hydrocarbons.

- Alkenes turn bromine water from orange to colourless.

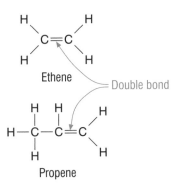

Ethene

Double bond

Propene

A molecule of ethene and a molecule of propene. These are both alkenes – each molecule has a carbon–carbon double bond in it.

- Large hydrocarbon molecules can be broken down into smaller molecules by a process called **cracking**.

- Cracking can be done in two ways:
  - by heating a mixture of hydrocarbon vapours and steam to a very high temperature
  - by passing hydrocarbon vapours over a hot catalyst.

- During cracking thermal decomposition reactions produce a mixture of smaller molecules. Some of the smaller molecules are alkanes, which are saturated hydrocarbons with the general formula C_nH_{2n+2}. These alkanes with smaller molecules are more useful as fuels.

▶ **1** *Give one reason why an oil company might want to crack large hydrocarbons to make smaller alkanes.*

- Some of the other smaller molecules formed are hydrocarbons with the general formula C_nH_{2n}. These are called **alkenes**. Alkenes are **unsaturated hydrocarbons** because they contain fewer hydrogen atoms than alkanes with the same number of carbon atoms.

$$C_{10}H_{22} \xrightarrow{800\,°C + catalyst} C_5H_{12} + C_3H_6 + C_2H_4$$
decane   pentane   propene   ethene

An example of a cracking reaction

- Alkenes have a **double bond** between two carbon atoms and this makes them more reactive than alkanes. Alkenes react with bromine water turning it from orange to colourless.

▶ **2** *Give three ways in which alkenes are different from alkanes.*

AQA *Examiner's tip*

Different mixtures of alkanes and alkenes can be produced by cracking because different hydrocarbons can be used and the conditions for the reaction can be changed.

Key words: cracking, alkene, unsaturated hydrocarbon, double bond

In an oil refinery huge crackers like this are used to break down large hydrocarbon molecules into smaller ones

5.2 Making polymers from alkenes

Containers like these are made from poly(ethene) and poly(propene)

AQA Examiner's tip

Double bonds in the monomer become single bonds in the polymer when the molecules have joined together.

- Plastics are made of very large molecules called **polymers**. Polymers are made from many small molecules joined together. The small molecules used to make polymers are called **monomers**. The reaction to make a polymer is called **polymerisation**.

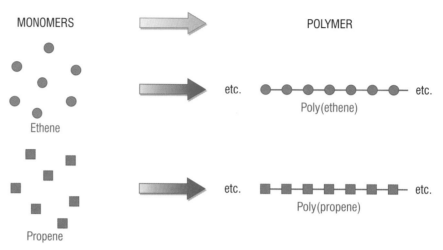

MONOMERS

POLYMER

etc. Poly(ethene) etc.

Ethene

etc. Poly(propene) etc.

Propene

Polymers are made from many smaller molecules called monomers

▶ **1** *How are polymers made?*

- Lots of **ethene** (C_2H_4) molecules can join together to form poly(ethene), commonly called polythene. In the polymerisation reaction the double bond in each ethene molecule becomes a single bond and thousands of ethene molecules join together in long chains.

Many single ethene monomers

Long chain of poly(ethene)

where *n* is a large number

▶ **2** *How many monomers are there in a poly(ethene) molecule?*

- Other alkenes can polymerise in a similar way. For example, **propene** (C_3H_6), can form poly(propene).

- Many of the plastics we use as bags, bottles, containers and toys are made from alkenes.

▶ **3** *Why can we make polymers from alkenes but not from alkanes?*

Bump up your grade

Learn to recognise monomers and polymers from diagrams. You should be able to draw the structure of the polymer made from a given monomer.

Key words: polymer, monomer, polymerisation, ethene, propene

5.3 New and useful polymers

- New polymers are being developed all the time.
- Polymers are designed to have properties that make them specially suited for certain uses.
- We are now recycling more plastics and finding new uses for them.

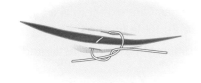

A shape-memory polymer uses the temperature of the body to make the thread tighten and close the wound

Recycling bottles like these can produce fibres for clothes or duvets

- Materials scientists can design new polymers to make materials with special properties for particular uses. Many of these materials are used for packaging, clothing and medical applications.

- New polymer materials for dental fillings have been developed to replace fillings that contain mercury. Light-sensitive polymers are used in sticking plasters to cover wounds so the plasters can be easily removed. Hydrogels are polymers that can trap water and have many uses including dressings for wounds.

- Shape-memory polymers change back to their original shape when temperature or other conditions are changed. An example of this type of **smart polymer** is a material used for stitching wounds that changes shape when heated to body temperature.

> **1** *What is a shape-memory polymer?*

- The fibres used to make fabrics can be coated with polymers to make them waterproof and breathable.

- The plastic used to make many drinks bottles can be recycled to make polyester fibres for clothing as well as filling pillows and duvets.

> **2** *Give two medical uses and two non-medical uses for polymers.*

AQA Examiner's tip

You should know some of the ways that polymers are used but you do not have to remember the names of specific polymers.

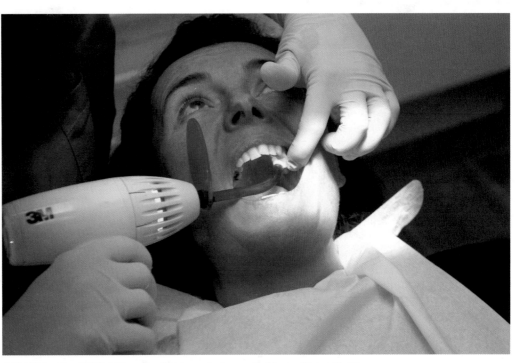

A dentist using UV light to set a filling made from a light-sensitive polymer

Key word: smart polymer

Student Book
pages 80–81

C1

5.4 Plastic waste

Key points

- Non-biodegradable plastics cause unsightly rubbish, can harm wildlife and take up space in landfill sites.
- Biodegradable plastics are decomposed by the action of microorganisms in soil.
- Making plastics with starch granules in their structure helps the microorganisms break down a plastic.
- We can make biodegradable plastics from plant material such as cornstarch.

- Many polymers are not **biodegradable**. This means that plastic waste is not broken down when left in the environment. Unless disposed of properly, plastic rubbish gets everywhere. It is unsightly and can harm wildlife. Even when put into landfill sites it takes up valuable space.
- We are using more plastics that are biodegradable. Microorganisms can break down biodegradable plastics. These plastics break down when in contact with soil.

▶ **1** *How would using biodegradable plastics help with the problems of plastic litter?*

- Plastics made from non-biodegradable polymers can have cornstarch mixed into the plastic. Microorganisms break down the cornstarch so the plastic breaks down into very small pieces that can be mixed with soil or compost.
- Biodegradable plastics can be made from plant material. One example is a polymer made from cornstarch that is used as biodegradable food packaging.
- Some plastics can be recycled but there are many different types of plastic and sorting is difficult.

▶ **2** *Describe the two ways that cornstarch can be used to help with problems of disposal of plastic waste.*

Key word: biodegradable

Student Book
pages 82–83

C1

5.5 Ethanol

Key points

- Ethanol can be made by fermenting sugar using enzymes in yeast.
- Ethanol can also be made by hydration of ethene with steam in the presence of a catalyst.
- Using ethene to make ethanol needs non-renewable crude oil whereas fermentation uses renewable plant material.

- Ethanol has the formula C_2H_6O. It is often written as C_2H_5OH. This shows the OH group in the molecule and that means it is an alcohol.
- Ethanol can be produced by the **fermentation** of sugar from plants using yeast.
- Enzymes in the yeast cause the sugar to convert to ethanol and carbon dioxide. This method is used to make alcoholic drinks.

▶ **1** *Write a word equation for the fermentation of sugar using yeast.*

- Ethanol can also be made by the hydration of ethene.
- Ethene is reacted with steam at a high temperature in the presence of a catalyst. The ethene is obtained from crude oil by cracking.

▶ **2** *Write a word equation for the hydration of ethene.*

- Ethanol produced by fermentation uses a renewable resource, sugar from plants.
- Fermentation is done at room temperature. However, fermentation can only produce a dilute aqueous solution of ethanol. The ethanol must be separated from the solution by fractional distillation to give pure ethanol.
- Ethanol produced from ethene uses a non-renewable resource, crude oil.
- The reaction can be run continuously and produces pure ethanol, but requires a high temperature.

Key word: fermentation

Bump up your grade

You should be able to describe the two ways of making ethanol and write balanced symbol equations for the reactions.

1 Give two reasons why fractions from crude oil are cracked.

2 Describe two ways that are used to crack hydrocarbons.

3 Sort these formulae into alkanes and alkenes:

C_3H_6, C_5H_{12}, C_4H_{10}, C_4H_8, C_6H_{14}

4 Poly(ethene) is a polymer. Explain what is meant by 'a polymer'.

5 Describe one use of a smart polymer.

6 Some plastics are biodegradable. What does 'biodegradable' mean?

7 Suggest three ways of reducing the problems of plastic rubbish.

8 Outline the two ways that can be used to make ethanol and give an advantage and a disadvantage of each method.

9 a Write an equation using displayed formulae showing the bonds for the polymerisation of propene.

  b Write a balanced equation showing the hydration of ethene. [H]

10 Copy and complete this equation for cracking a hydrocarbon:

$C_{12}H_{26} \rightarrow C_6H_{14} + C_4H_8 +$ ……… [H]

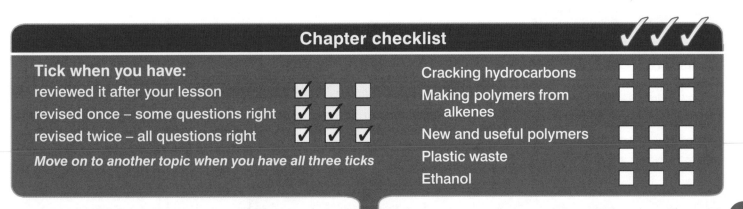

Chapter checklist	✓ ✓ ✓

Tick when you have:

reviewed it after your lesson	✓	☐	☐	Cracking hydrocarbons	☐	☐	☐
revised once – some questions right	✓	✓	☐	Making polymers from alkenes	☐	☐	☐
revised twice – all questions right	✓	✓	✓	New and useful polymers	☐	☐	☐
Move on to another topic when you have all three ticks				Plastic waste	☐	☐	☐
				Ethanol	☐	☐	☐

Student Book
pages 86–87 **C1**

6.1 Extracting vegetable oil

● Some seeds, nuts and fruits are rich in **vegetable oils**. The oils can be extracted by crushing and pressing the plant material, followed by removing water and other impurities. Some oils are extracted by distilling the plant material mixed with water. This produces a mixture of oil and water from which the oil can be separated.

➤ 1 *What two methods are used to extract vegetable oils?*

● When eaten, vegetable oils provide us with a lot of energy and important nutrients. Vegetable oils also release a lot of energy when they burn in air and so can be used as fuels. They are used to make biofuels such as biodiesel.

➤ 2 *Why are vegetable oils important foods?*

● The molecules in vegetable oils have hydrocarbon chains. Those with carbon–carbon double bonds (C=C) are unsaturated. If there are several double bonds in each molecule, they are called polyunsaturated. **Unsaturated oils** react with bromine water, turning it from orange to colourless.

➤ 3 *Why are some vegetable oils described as unsaturated?*

Key words: vegetable oil, unsaturated oil

Student Book
pages 88–89 **C1**

6.2 Cooking with vegetable oils

● The boiling points of vegetable oils are higher than water, so food is cooked at higher temperatures in oil. This means it cooks faster. It also changes the flavour, colour and texture of the food. Some of the oil is absorbed and so the energy content of the food increases.

➤ 1 *Why are many of the foods from fast food outlets cooked in oil?*

Unsaturated oils can be reacted with hydrogen so that some or all of the carbon–carbon double bonds become single bonds. This reaction is called hydrogenation and is done at about 60°C using a nickel catalyst. The **hydrogenated oils** have higher melting points because they are more saturated. The reaction is also called **hardening** because the hydrogenated oils are solids at room temperature. This means they can be used as spreads and to make pastries and cakes that require solid fats.

➤ 2 *What is meant by hardening vegetable oils?*

AQA **Examiner's tip**

Increasing the temperature makes chemical reactions go faster, so food cooks faster in oil than in water.

Key words: hydrogenated oil, hardening

Student Book
pages 90–91

C1

Key points

- Oils do not dissolve in water but oils and water can be used to produce emulsions. These have special properties.
- Emulsions made from vegetable oils are used in many foods.
- Emulsifiers stop oil and water from separating into layers.
- Emulsifiers have molecules in which one part is hydrophobic and one part is hydrophilic. **[H]**

Ice cream is a frozen emulsifier

Bump up your grade

Try to describe how an emulsifier works using the words 'hydrophobic' and 'hydrophilic'.

6.3 Everyday emulsions

- Oil and water do not mix and usually separate from each other, forming two layers. If we shake, stir or beat the liquids together tiny droplets form that can be slow to separate. This type of mixture is called an **emulsion**.

- Emulsions are opaque and thicker than the oil and water they are made from. This improves their texture, appearance and their ability to coat and stick to solids. Milk, cream, salad dressings and ice cream are examples of emulsions. Some water-based paints and many cosmetic creams are also emulsions.

▶ **1** *How can you recognise an emulsion?*

- **Emulsifiers** are substances that help stop the oil and water from separating into layers. Most emulsions contain emulsifiers to keep the emulsion stable.

Higher

Emulsifier molecules have a small **hydrophilic** part and a long **hydrophobic** part. The hydrophilic part or 'head' is attracted to water. The hydrophobic part or 'tail' is attracted to oil. The hydrophobic parts of many emulsifier molecules go into each oil droplet, and so the droplets become surrounded by the hydrophilic parts. This keeps the droplets apart in the water, preventing them from joining together and separating out.

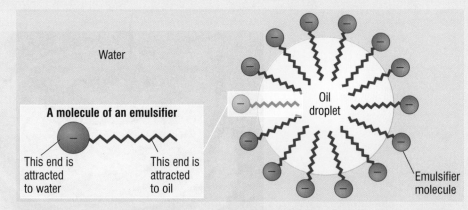

The structure of a typical emulsifier molecule with its water-loving (hydrophilic) head and its water-hating (hydrophobic) tail

▶ **2** *What is an emulsifier?*

AQA Examiner's tip

You cannot see through an emulsion because the liquids remain as tiny droplets and do not dissolve. In a solution the substances dissolve, which means they mix completely, and the solution is clear.

Key words: emulsion, emulsifier, hydrophilic, hydrophobic

6.4 Food issues

- There are benefits and drawbacks to using vegetable oils and emulsifiers in foods.
- Vegetable oils are high in energy and contain important nutrients. They contain unsaturated fats that are believed to be better for your health than saturated fats.
- Animal fats and hydrogenated vegetable oils contain saturated fats and are used in many foods. Saturated fats have been linked to heart disease.
- Emulsifiers stop oil and water separating into layers. This makes foods smoother, creamier and more palatable. However, because they taste better and it is less obvious that they are high in fat, you may be tempted to eat more.

> 1 *Give one benefit and one drawback from eating foods that contain vegetable oils.*
> 2 *Why should you be aware of emulsifiers in the food you eat?*

AQA *Examiner's tip*

You should be aware of the issues in this section to help you answer questions about information you are given in the exam, but you do not need to remember names of specific fats, oils or emulsifiers.

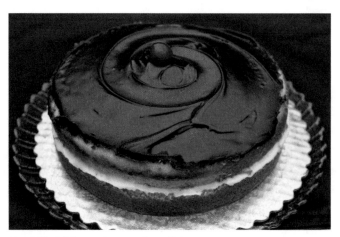

Emulsified fats can be very tempting

1 Why are vegetable oils used as food and fuels?

2 What type of fuel is produced from vegetable oils?

3 What is used to test for an unsaturated oil? Give the result of the test.

4 Why are some foods cooked in vegetable oils?

5 Describe how to make an emulsion from cooking oil and water.

6 Mayonnaise is made from oil, vinegar and egg yolk. What is the purpose of the egg yolk?

7 Why are emulsions more useful than separate oil and water?

8 Why should you know what type of fats are in the food you eat?

9 Sunflower seeds contain vegetable oil. Outline a method you could use to separate some oil from the seeds.

10 a Describe the reaction and conditions used to hydrogenate vegetable oils.

    b Why is this done? [H]

11 Describe how an emulsifier works. [H]

Chapter checklist	✓ ✓ ✓

Tick when you have:							
reviewed it after your lesson	✓	☐	☐	Extracting vegetable oil	☐	☐	☐
revised once – some questions right	✓	✓	☐	Cooking with vegetable oils	☐	☐	☐
revised twice – all questions right	✓	✓	✓	Everyday emulsions	☐	☐	☐
				Food issues	☐	☐	☐

Move on to another topic when you have all three ticks

Student Book
pages 96–97

C1

7.1 Structure of the Earth

Key points

- The Earth is made of layers called the core, mantle and crust with the atmosphere around the outside.

- The Earth's limited resources come from its crust, the oceans and the atmosphere.

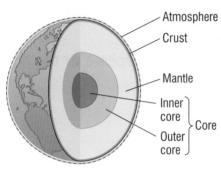

The structure of the Earth

- The Earth is almost spherical, with a diameter of about 12 800 km. At the surface is a thin, solid **crust**. The crust is a very thin layer that varies in thickness between about 5 km and 70 km.

- The **mantle** is under the crust and is about 3000 km thick. It goes almost halfway to the centre of the Earth. The mantle is almost entirely solid but parts of it can flow very slowly.

- The **core** is about half the diameter of the Earth. It has a high proportion of the magnetic metals iron and nickel. It has a liquid outer part and a solid inner part.

- The **atmosphere** surrounds the Earth. Most of the air is within 10 km of the surface and most of the atmosphere is within 100 km of the surface.

⫸ **1** *Name the layers of the Earth that are solid.*

- All of the raw materials and other resources that we depend on come from the crust, the oceans and the atmosphere. This means the resources available to us are limited.

AQA Examiner's tip

You should have an idea of the size of the Earth and the relative size of its layers. You do not have to remember the diameter or thickness of the layers.

Key words: crust, mantle, core, atmosphere

Student Book
pages 98–99

C1

7.2 The restless Earth

Key points

- The Earth's crust and upper mantle is cracked into tectonic plates which are constantly moving.

- The tectonic plates move because of convection currents in the mantle that are caused by radioactive decay.

- Earthquakes and volcanoes happen where tectonic plates meet, but it is difficult to predict accurately when and where earthquakes will happen.

- Wegener's theory of continental drift was not accepted for many years.

- Scientists now believe the Earth's crust and upper part of the mantle is cracked into massive pieces called **tectonic plates**. Tectonic plates move a few centimetres a year because of **convection currents** in the mantle beneath them. The convection currents are caused by energy released by the decay of radioactive elements heating up the mantle.

⫸ **1** *What causes tectonic plates to move?*

- Where the plates meet, huge forces build up. Eventually the rocks give way, changing shape or moving suddenly causing earthquakes, volcanoes or mountains to form. Scientists still do not know enough about what is happening inside the Earth to predict exactly when and where earthquakes or volcanic eruptions will happen.

⫸ **2** *Why can scientists not predict when and where earthquakes will happen?*

- Alfred Wegener put forward the idea of continental drift in 1915. Other scientists at that time did not accept his ideas, mainly because he could not explain why the continents moved. They believed that the Earth was shrinking as it cooled. In the 1960s scientists found new evidence and the theory of plate tectonics was developed.

⫸ **3** *Why were Wegener's ideas not accepted for many years?*

Bump up your grade

You should be able to explain how and why tectonic plates move.

Key words: tectonic plate, convection current

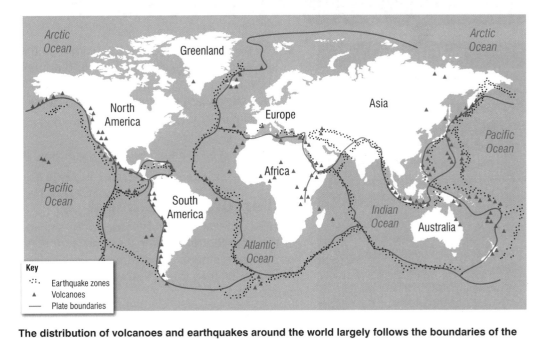

Key	
:..:	Earthquake zones
▲	Volcanoes
—	Plate boundaries

The distribution of volcanoes and earthquakes around the world largely follows the boundaries of the Earth's tectonic plates

Student Book pages 100–101 **C1**

7.3 The Earth's atmosphere in the past

Key points

- The Earth's early atmosphere was formed by volcanic activity.
- It probably consisted mainly of carbon dioxide. There may also have been water vapour together with traces of methane and ammonia.
- As plants spread over the Earth, the levels of oxygen in the atmosphere increased

- Scientists think that the Earth was formed about 4.5 billion years ago. In the first billion years the surface was covered with volcanoes that released carbon dioxide, water vapour and nitrogen.

- As the Earth cooled most of the water vapour condensed to form the oceans. So the early atmosphere was mainly carbon dioxide with some water vapour. Some scientists believe there was also nitrogen and possibly some methane and ammonia.

> ▶ 1 *Where did most of the carbon dioxide, nitrogen and water vapour in the Earth's early atmosphere come from?*

- In the next two billion years bacteria, algae and plants evolved. Algae and plants used carbon dioxide for photosynthesis and this released oxygen. As the number of plants increased the amount of carbon dioxide in the atmosphere decreased and the amount of oxygen increased.

> ▶ 2 *What produced the oxygen in the atmosphere?*

 Examiner's tip

You may find other theories about the Earth's formation and its early atmosphere, but you are only expected to know about this one for the examination.

Bump up your grade

Try to memorise the main gases that were probably in the Earth's early atmosphere.

The surface of one of Jupiter's moons, called Io, with its active volcanoes releasing gases into its atmosphere. This gives us an idea of what our Earth was like billions of years ago.

7.4 Life on Earth

- The plants that produced the oxygen in the atmosphere probably evolved from simple organisms like plankton and algae in the ancient oceans. But we do not know how the molecules of the simplest living things were formed. Many scientists have suggested theories of how life began but no one knows for sure because we have insufficient evidence.

1 *Why are we not sure about how life began?*

Miller–Urey experiment

In 1952 two scientists, Miller and Urey, did an experiment based on what scientists at that time thought was in the early atmosphere. They used a mixture of water, ammonia, methane and hydrogen and a high voltage spark to simulate lightning. After a week they found that amino acids, the building blocks for proteins, had been produced.

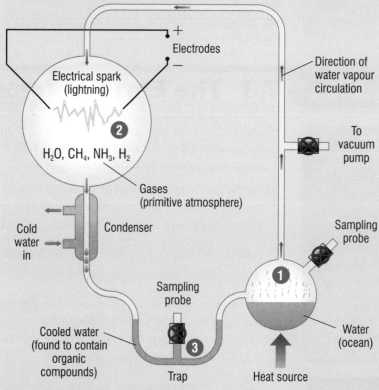

The classic Miller–Urey experiment

Other theories

Since the 1950s theories about what was in the early atmosphere have changed, but scientists have been able to produce amino acids using other mixtures of gases. One theory suggests that these organic molecules formed a 'primordial soup' and that the amino acids in this mixture combined to make proteins from which life began. Many other theories have been proposed, but there is no evidence that proves any theory.

2 *Amino acids are made from the elements carbon, hydrogen, oxygen and nitrogen. Suggest why Miller and Urey used a mixture of water, ammonia, methane and hydrogen in their experiment.*

Key points

- There are many theories about how life began on Earth.

- One theory states that the compounds needed came from reactions involving hydrocarbons and ammonia with lightning providing energy.   [H]

- All the theories about how life started on Earth are unproven and so we cannot be sure how life began.   [H]

AQA Examiner's tip

Although there are many theories about how life began you do not need to remember the details of any of them, except for Higher Tier candidates, who should be aware of the Miller–Urey experiment and the idea of 'primordial soup'.

Student Book
pages 104–105 **C1**

7.5 Gases in the atmosphere

- Plants took up much of the carbon dioxide in the Earth's early atmosphere. Animals ate the plants and much of the carbon ended up in plant and animal remains as sedimentary rocks and fossil fuels. Limestone was formed from the shells and skeletons of marine organisms. Fossil fuels contain carbon and hydrogen from plants and animals.

- Carbon dioxide dissolves in the oceans and some probably formed insoluble carbonate compounds that were deposited on the seabed and became sedimentary rocks.

1 *In what ways did carbon from carbon dioxide become 'locked up'?*

- By 200 million years ago the proportions of gases in the atmosphere had stabilised and were much the same as today. The atmosphere is now almost four-fifths nitrogen and just over one-fifth oxygen. Other gases, including carbon dioxide, water vapour and noble gases, make up about 1% of the atmosphere.

2 *What are the approximate percentages of nitrogen and oxygen in the air?*

Key points

- Most of the carbon dioxide in the early atmosphere became locked up in sedimentary rocks.

- About four-fifths (almost 80%) of the atmosphere is nitrogen, and about one-fifth (just over 20%) is oxygen.

- The main gases in the air can be separated by fractional distillation. These gases are used in industry as raw materials. **[H]**

Separating the gases in air

The gases in the air have different boiling points and so can be separated from liquid air by **fractional distillation**. Fractional distillation of liquid air is done industrially to produce pure oxygen and liquid nitrogen, which have important uses. The air is cooled to below −200 °C and fed into a fractional distillation column. Nitrogen is separated from oxygen and argon and further distillation is used to produce pure oxygen and argon.

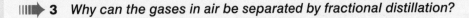

3 *Why can the gases in air be separated by fractional distillation?*

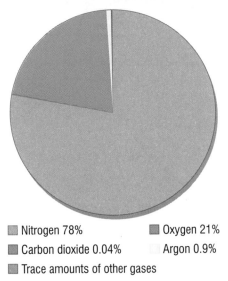

- Nitrogen 78%
- Oxygen 21%
- Carbon dioxide 0.04%
- Argon 0.9%
- Trace amounts of other gases

The relative proportions of nitrogen, oxygen and other gases in the Earth's atmosphere

Bump up your grade

To get maximum marks, you should be able to explain the fractional distillation of liquid air, given the boiling points of nitrogen and oxygen.

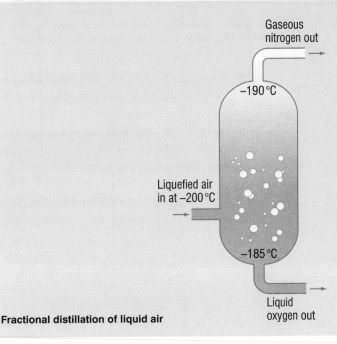

Gaseous nitrogen out

−190 °C

Liquefied air in at −200 °C

−185 °C

Liquid oxygen out

Fractional distillation of liquid air

Higher

7.6 Carbon dioxide in the atmosphere

Key points

- Carbon moves into and out of the atmosphere due to plants, animals, the oceans and rocks.

- The amount of carbon dioxide in the Earth's atmosphere has risen in the recent past largely due to the amount of fossil fuels we now burn.

AQA *Examiner's tip*

Questions on this topic will test your understanding of the main processes that add or remove carbon dioxide and how they affect its amount in the atmosphere. You only need to know those included in the AQA specification. There are other processes involved, and you may be given information about these in the exam, but you will not be expected to remember their details.

- For about 200 million years the amount of carbon dioxide in the atmosphere has remained about the same.

- This is because various natural processes that move carbon dioxide into and out of the atmosphere had achieved a balance.

- These processes involve carbon compounds in plants, animals, the oceans and rocks. The organic carbon cycle shows some of these processes.

- Carbon dioxide dissolves in water, particularly the oceans, and reactions of inorganic carbonate compounds are also important in maintaining a balance.

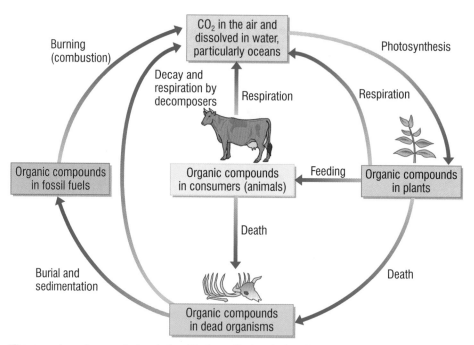

The organic carbon cycle has helped to keep the level of carbon dioxide in the atmosphere steady for the last 200 million years

> 1 *Name two processes that release carbon dioxide into the atmosphere and two processes that remove it from the atmosphere.*

- In the recent past the amount of carbon dioxide that human activity has released into the atmosphere has increased dramatically. This has been mainly caused by the large increase in the amount of fossil fuels that we burn.

> 2 *Which human activity has been the main cause of increased carbon dioxide levels in the atmosphere?*

1 Name the main parts of the Earth, starting from its centre.

2 Why should we be careful not to waste the Earth's resources?

3 Name three gases that scientists think were in the Earth's early atmosphere.

4 Name four gases that are now in the atmosphere.

5 How did the oceans form?

6 What was the effect of algae and plants on the early atmosphere?

7 a What are tectonic plates?

   b Why do tectonic plates move?

   c About how much do they move in a year?

   d What happens at plate boundaries?

8 a Why have the amounts of gases in the atmosphere been almost the same for the last 200 million years?

   b What has been the main cause of a change in this balance in recent years?

9 Why were Wegener's ideas not accepted until the 1960s?

10 Why are there so many theories about how life began?

11 a Outline the Miller and Urey experiment. [H]

   b What is meant by 'primordial soup'?

12 a Why is the fractional distillation of liquid air done commercially? [H]

   b Explain briefly how it works.

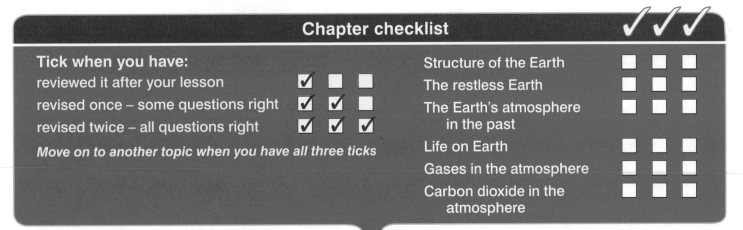

Chapter checklist

Tick when you have:				Structure of the Earth	☐	☐	☐
reviewed it after your lesson	✔	☐	☐	The restless Earth	☐	☐	☐
revised once – some questions right	✔	✔	☐	The Earth's atmosphere in the past	☐	☐	☐
revised twice – all questions right	✔	✔	✔	Life on Earth	☐	☐	☐
Move on to another topic when you have all three ticks				Gases in the atmosphere	☐	☐	☐
				Carbon dioxide in the atmosphere	☐	☐	☐

1 The symbol for the element phosphorus is P and its atomic number is 15.
  a How many protons are in an atom of phosphorus? *(1 mark)*

  b How many electrons are in an atom of phosphorus? *(1 mark)*

  c The mass number of an atom of phosphorus is 31. How many neutrons are in this atom? *(1 mark)*

  d Copy and complete the electronic structure of phosphorus: 2,8, ….. *(1 mark)*

  e In which group of the periodic table is phosphorus? *(1 mark)*

  f Phosphorus reacts with chlorine to form phosphorus chloride, PCl_3. The equation for the reaction is:

$$2P + 3Cl_2 \rightarrow 2PCl_3$$

  i Write a word equation for the reaction. *(1 mark)*

  ii How many atoms of chlorine combine with two atoms of phosphorus? *(1 mark)*

  iii What type of bond holds the atoms together in PCl_3? *(1 mark)*

2 Limestone is mainly calcium carbonate, $CaCO_3$.
  a When limestone is heated strongly the calcium carbonate breaks down.
  i Write a word equation for this reaction. *(1 mark)*
  ii What type of reaction is this? *(1 mark)*

  b When water is added to the solid product, calcium hydroxide, $Ca(OH)_2$, is produced. Adding more water and filtering produces a solution of calcium hydroxide.
  i Some universal indicator solution was added to calcium hydroxide solution. The indicator turned blue. What does this tell you about calcium hydroxide? *(1 mark)*

  ii When carbon dioxide is bubbled into calcium hydroxide solution the solution turns cloudy. Explain why. *(2 marks)*

3 a Copper can be extracted from copper-rich ores by smelting. This is done by heating the ore in a furnace to about 1100 °C and blowing air through it. An equation for a reaction in the furnace is:

copper sulfide + oxygen → copper + sulfur dioxide

  i Copper ore and air are needed for this process. What other resource is needed? *(1 mark)*

  ii Why should sulfur dioxide not be allowed to escape into the air? *(1 mark)*

  iii The copper that is produced is impure. Name the method used to purify the copper. *(1 mark)*

  b Copper can be extracted from low-grade ores by bioleaching. A solution containing water, bacteria and sulfuric acid is added to the top of a heap of ore. The leachate solution that is collected from the bottom of the heap contains copper sulfate. Copper is extracted from the solution using scrap iron. The solution can be re-used.
  i What is the purpose of the bacteria in this process? *(1 mark)*
  ii Write a word equation for the reaction between iron and copper sulfate. *(1 mark)*

  iii What is the name of this type of reaction? *(1 mark)*

  iv The solution from which the copper has been extracted should not be allowed to escape without further treatment. Explain why. *(2 marks)*

4 Oil companies crack some of the fractions from crude oil. The equation shows an example of a reaction that happens during cracking.

$$C_{12}H_{26} \rightarrow C_7H_{16} + C_2H_4 + C_3H_6$$

a What conditions are used for cracking? *(2 marks)*

b Draw a diagram to show all of the bonds in C_3H_6. *(2 marks)*

c C_3H_6 can be used to make a polymer. Which other product of the reaction can be used to make a polymer? *(1 mark)*

d *In this question you will be assessed on using good English, organising information clearly and using specialist terms where appropriate.*

Plastic waste that contains polymers made from C_3H_6 and similar monomers causes environmental problems. Explain why. *(6 marks)*

5 The table shows the percentages of the four most abundant gases in dry air.

Name of gas	Percentage (%) by volume in dry air
Nitrogen	78.08
Oxygen	20.95
Argon	0.93
Carbon dioxide	0.03

a Which of these gases is believed to have been the most abundant in the Earth's early atmosphere? *(1 mark)*

b Name **one** other gas that was probably in the Earth's early atmosphere. *(1 mark)*

c What produced the oxygen that is in the air? *(1 mark)*

d Why are there many theories about how life began on Earth? *(1 mark)*

e In the Miller–Urey experiment electric sparks were passed through a mixture of gases. The gases were those that scientists believed were in the early atmosphere. After several days amino acids were produced. The simplest amino acid has the formula $C_2H_5O_2N$. Suggest a mixture of three gases that could have been in the Earth's early atmosphere that could combine to form amino acids. **[H]** *(3 marks)*

f The table shows the boiling points of the three most abundant elements in air.

Name of element	Boiling point in °C
Argon	−186
Nitrogen	−196
Oxygen	−183

To separate these elements, air is cooled to −200°C, so that the gases become liquids. The liquid mixture is then put into a fractional distillation column that is colder at the bottom than the top. From which part of the column is each element is collected? **[H]** *(2 marks)*

Student Book
pages 112–113

C2

1.1 Chemical bonding

- When two or more elements react together compounds are formed. The atoms of elements join together by sharing electrons or by transferring electrons to achieve stable electronic structures. Atoms of the noble gases have stable electronic structures.
- When atoms of non-metallic elements join together by sharing electrons it is called **covalent bonding**.

▶ **1** *How can you tell that the compound H_2O has covalent bonds?*

- When metallic elements react with non-metallic elements they produce ionic compounds. The metal atoms lose electrons to form positive **ions**. The atoms of non-metals gain electrons to form negative ions. The ions have the stable electronic structure of a noble gas. The oppositely charged ions attract each other in the ionic compound and this is called **ionic bonding**.

▶ **2** *Which of these compounds have ionic bonding?*
  KBr, HCl, H_2S, Na_2O, Cl_2O, MgO

- Elements in Group 1 of the periodic table have atoms with one electron in their highest occupied energy level (outer shell). Sodium atoms, Na, (electronic structure 2,8,1), form sodium ions, Na^+ (electronic structure 2,8).
- Elements in Group 7 of the periodic table have atoms with seven electrons in their highest occupied energy level (outer shell). Chlorine atoms, Cl (2,8,7) form chloride ions, Cl^- (2,8,8).
- The compound sodium chloride has equal numbers of sodium ions and chloride ions and so we write its formula as NaCl.

▶ **3** *Explain what happens to the atoms of the elements when lithium reacts with fluorine.*

Key words: covalent bonding, ion, ionic bonding

Key points

- Elements react to form compounds by gaining or losing electrons, or by sharing electrons.
- Atoms of metals in Group 1 combine with atoms of non-metals in Group 7 by transferring electrons to form ions that have the electronic structures of noble gases.

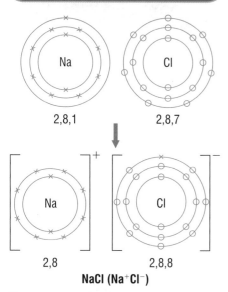

2,8,1   2,8,7

2,8   2,8,8

NaCl (Na^+Cl^-)

The formation of sodium chloride (NaCl) is an example of ion formation by transferring an electron

Student Book
pages 114–115

C2

1.2 Ionic bonding

- Ionic bonding holds oppositely charged ions together in **giant structures**. The giant structure of ionic compounds is very regular because the ions all pack together neatly, like marbles in a box.
- Strong electrostatic forces of attraction act in all directions. Each ion in the giant structure or lattice is surrounded by ions with the opposite charge and so is held firmly in place.
- Sodium chloride contains equal numbers of sodium ions and chloride ions as shown by its formula NaCl. The sodium ions and chloride ions alternate to form a cubic lattice.
- The ratio of ions in the structure of an ionic compound depends on the charges on the ions. For example, calcium ions are Ca^{2+} and chloride ions are Cl^-, so calcium chloride contains twice as many chloride ions as calcium ions and its formula is $CaCl_2$.

Key points

- Ionic compounds are held together by strong forces between the oppositely charged ions. This is called ionic bonding.
- The ions form a giant structure or lattice. The strong forces of attraction act throughout the lattice.
- We can represent atoms and ions using dot and cross diagrams.

All ionic compounds have giant structures, but you do not need to know the shapes of any structures other than sodium chloride.

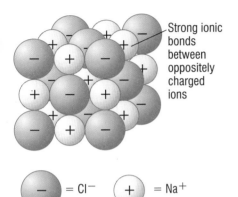

Strong ionic bonds between oppositely charged ions

— = Cl⁻   + = Na⁺

Part of the giant ionic lattice (3D-network) of sodium and chloride ions in sodium chloride

▶ **1** Why is the formula of sodium chloride NaCl but magnesium chloride is $MgCl_2$?

● We can use **dot and cross diagrams** to represent the atoms and ions involved in forming ionic bonds. In these diagrams we only show the electrons in the outermost shell of each atom or ion.

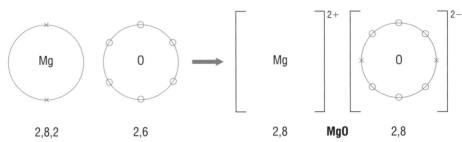

2,8,2   2,6   2,8   **MgO**   2,8

When magnesium oxide (MgO) is formed, the reacting magnesium atoms lose two electrons and the oxygen atoms gain two electrons

▶ **2** Draw a dot and cross diagram to show sodium atoms and chlorine atoms form ions.

Key words: giant structure or lattice, dot and cross diagram

Student Book
pages 116–117   **C2**

1.3 Formulae of ionic compounds

Key points

● The charges on the ions in an ionic compound always cancel each other out.

● The formula of an ionic compound shows the ratio of ions present in the compound.

● Sometimes we need brackets to show the ratio of ions in a compound, e.g. magnesium hydroxide, $Mg(OH)_2$.

● Ionic compounds are neutral. If we know the charge on each ion in a compound we can work out its formula by balancing the charges. Sodium chloride is NaCl (one Na^+ ion for every one Cl^- ion), but calcium chloride is $CaCl_2$ (one Ca^{2+} ion for every two Cl^- ions).

● The charge on simple ions formed by elements in the main groups of the periodic table can be worked out from the number of the group. For transition metals the charge on the ion is shown by the Roman numeral in the name of the compound, for example iron(II) sulfate contains Fe^{2+}. In the examination you will have a data sheet showing the charges of ions.

● Some ions are made up of more than one element, for example carbonate ions are CO_3^{2-} and hydroxide ions are OH^-. If we need to multiply these ions to write a formula we use brackets. The formula of calcium carbonate is $CaCO_3$, and the formula of calcium hydroxide is $Ca(OH)_2$.

▶ **1** Write the formula for each of these compounds:
calcium fluoride, sodium sulfate, magnesium nitrate, copper(II) chloride, iron(III) hydroxide.

▲ **Bump up your grade**

Make sure you can write the correct formula for any compound from the ions on the data sheet.

Do not forget that ionic compounds are giant structures. The formula of an ionic compound is the simplest ratio of the ions in the compound and does not represent a molecule.

1.4 Covalent bonding

- The atoms of non-metals need to gain electrons to achieve stable electronic structures. They can do this by sharing electrons with other atoms. Each shared pair of electrons strongly attracts the two atoms, forming a covalent bond. Substances that have atoms held together by covalent bonding are called molecules.

- Atoms of elements in Group 7 need to gain one electron and so form a single covalent bond. Atoms of elements in Group 6 need to gain two electrons and so form two covalent bonds. Atoms of elements in Group 5 can form three bonds and those in Group 4 can form four bonds.

- A covalent bond acts only between the two atoms it bonds to each other, and so many covalently bonded substances consist of small molecules. Some atoms that can form several bonds, like carbon, can join together in giant covalent structures. These giant covalent structures are sometimes referred to as macromolecules.

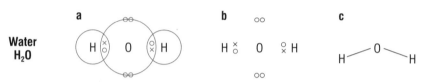

Water H_2O

a   **b**   **c**

We can represent a covalent compound by showing electrons or using lines for covalent bonds

Key points

- A covalent bond is formed when two atoms share a pair of electrons.
- The number of covalent bonds an atom forms depends on the number of electrons it needs to achieve a stable electronic structure.
- Many substances containing covalent bonds consist of simple molecules, but some have giant covalent structures.

AQA **Examiner's tip**

Covalent bonds join atoms together to form molecules. You should only use the word molecule when describing substances that are covalently bonded.

▎▶ **1** *Draw diagrams using symbols and lines to show the covalent bonds in: chlorine Cl$_2$, hydrogen chloride HCl, hydrogen sulfide H$_2$S, oxygen O$_2$, and carbon dioxide CO$_2$.*

1.5 Metals

- The atoms in a metallic element are all the same size. They form giant structures in which layers of atoms are arranged in regular patterns. You can make models of metal structures by putting lots of small same-sized spheres like marbles together.

▎▶ **1** *How are the atoms arranged in a metal?*

Key points

- The atoms in metals are closely packed together and arranged in regular layers.
- The electrons in the highest energy level are delocalised. The strong electrostatic forces between these electrons and the positively charged metal ions hold the metal together. **[H]**

Metallic bonding

When metal atoms pack together the electrons in the highest energy level (the outer electrons) delocalise and can move freely between atoms. This produces a lattice of positive ions in a 'sea' of moving electrons. The **delocalised electrons** strongly attract the positive ions and hold the giant structure together.

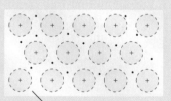

The 'sea' of delocalised electrons

▎▶ **2** *What forces hold metal atoms in place in their giant structures?*

Key word: delocalised electron

The close-packed arrangement of copper atoms in copper metal

1 What is a compound?

2 a Which electrons in an atom are involved in bonding?

b What happens to the electrons in atoms when ionic bonds are formed?

c What happens to electrons in atoms when covalent bonds are formed?

3 a Why do the elements in Group 1 form ions with a single positive charge?

b Why do the elements in Group 7 form ions with a single negative charge?

4 Which of the following substances are made of molecules?
KCl, H_2O, C_2H_6, MgO, CO_2, $NaNO_3$.

5 Why can the structure of a metallic element like copper be represented by lots of small spheres the same size packed together?

6 Write the correct formula for each of the following: lithium chloride, sodium oxide, calcium fluoride, magnesium hydroxide, sodium sulfate, calcium nitrate.

7 Why do ionic compounds have giant structures?

8 Draw a dot and cross diagram to show the bonding in methane, CH_4.

9 Draw diagrams using symbols and lines to show the covalent bonds in F_2, O_2, HBr, H_2O, NH_3.

10 Draw dot and cross diagrams to show what happens when a potassium atom reacts with a fluorine atom.

11 Explain why silicon (in Group 4) has a giant structure.

12 Explain how the atoms in a piece of sodium metal are held together. [H]

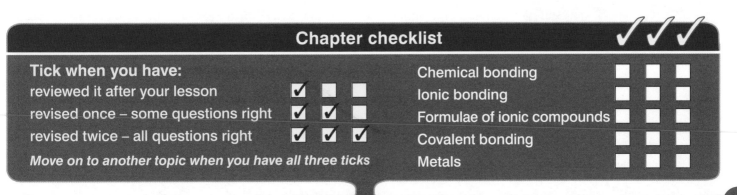

Chapter checklist						
Tick when you have:				Chemical bonding		
reviewed it after your lesson	✓	☐	☐	Ionic bonding		
revised once – some questions right	✓	✓	☐	Formulae of ionic compounds		
revised twice – all questions right	✓	✓	✓	Covalent bonding		
Move on to another topic when you have all three ticks				Metals		

Student Book
pages 124–125 **C2**

2.1 Giant ionic structures

- Ionic compounds have giant structures in which many strong electrostatic forces hold the ions together. This means they are solids at room temperature. A lot of energy is needed to overcome the ionic bonds to melt the solids. Therefore ionic compounds have high melting points and high boiling points.

▊▶ **1** *Why do ionic solids have high melting points?*

- However, when an ionic compound has been melted the ions are free to move. This allows them to carry electrical charge, so the liquids conduct electricity. Some ionic solids dissolve in water because water molecules can split up the lattice. The ions are free to move in the solutions and so they also conduct electricity.

▊▶ **2** *Why can ionic substances conduct electricity when molten or when dissolved in water?*

Key points

- Ionic compounds have high melting points and they are all solids at room temperature.
- Ionic compounds will conduct electricity when we melt them or dissolve them in water. Their ions can then move freely and can carry charge through the liquid.

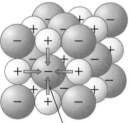

The attractive forces in an ionic compound are very strong

Strong electrostatic forces of attraction called ionic bonds

AQA *Examiner's tip*

Ionic compounds cannot conduct electricity when solid because the ions can only vibrate about fixed positions; they cannot move around. The compound must be melted or dissolved in water for the ions to be able to move about freely.

Student Book
pages 126–127 **C2**

2.2 Simple molecules

- The atoms within a molecule are held together by strong covalent bonds. These bonds act only between the atoms within the molecule, and so simple molecules have little attraction for each other. Substances made of simple molecules have relatively low melting points and boiling points. They do not conduct electricity because molecules have no overall charge and so cannot carry electrical charge.

▊▶ **1** *Why does petrol not conduct electricity?*

Key points

- Substances made up of simple molecules have low melting points and boiling points.
- Simple molecules have no overall charge, so they cannot carry electrical charge and do not conduct electricity.
- The weak intermolecular forces between simple molecules are why substances made of simple molecules have low melting points and boiling points. [H]

Intermolecular forces

The forces of attraction between molecules, called **intermolecular forces**, are weak. These forces are overcome when a molecular substance melts or boils. This means that substances made of small molecules have low melting and boiling points. Those with the smallest molecules, like H_2, Cl_2 and CH_4, have the weakest intermolecular forces and are gases at room temperature. Larger molecules have stronger attractions and so may be liquids at room temperature, like Br_2 and C_6H_{14}, or solids with low melting points, like I_2.

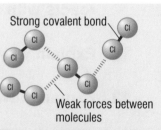

Strong covalent bond

Weak forces between molecules

There are weak intermolecular forces between chlorine molecules

▊▶ **2** *Why are substances with large molecules more likely to be liquids or solids at room temperature?*

Key word: intermolecular force

2.3 Giant covalent structures

- Atoms of some elements can form several covalent bonds. These atoms can join together in **giant covalent structures** (sometimes called **macromolecules**). Every atom in the structure is joined to several other atoms by strong covalent bonds. It takes an enormous amount of energy to break down the lattice and so these substances have very high melting points.

▶ **1** *Why do substances with giant covalent structures have very high melting points?*

- Diamond is a form of carbon that has a regular three-dimensional giant structure. Every carbon atom is covalently bonded to four other carbon atoms. This makes diamond hard and transparent. The compound silicon dioxide (silica) has a similar structure.

- Graphite is a form of carbon in which the atoms are covalently bonded to three other carbon atoms in giant flat two-dimensional layers. There are no covalent bonds between the layers and so they slide over each other, making graphite slippery and grey.

▶ **2** *Give two similarities and two differences between diamond and graphite.*

Key points

- Covalently bonded substances with giant structures have very high melting points.
- Diamond is a form of carbon whose atoms each form four covalent bonds.
- Graphite is another form of carbon where the carbon atoms form layers that can slide over each other.
- Graphite can conduct electricity because of the delocalised electrons in its structure. **[H]**
- Carbon also exists as fullerenes. **[H]**

Bonding in graphite and fullerenes

In graphite each carbon atom bonds covalently to three other carbon atoms forming a flat sheet of hexagons. One electron from each carbon atom is delocalised, rather like electrons in a metal. These **delocalised electrons** allow graphite to conduct heat and electricity.

There are only weak intermolecular forces between the layers in graphite, so the layers can slide over each other quite easily.

Fullerenes are large molecules formed from hexagonal rings of carbon atoms. The rings join together to form cage-like shapes with different numbers of carbon atoms, some of which are nano-sized. Scientists are finding many applications for fullerenes, including drug delivery into the body, lubricants, catalysts and reinforcing materials.

▶ **3** *Give two similarities and one difference between graphite and fullerenes.*

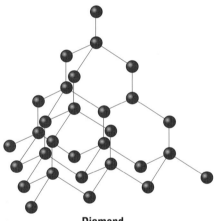

Diamond

The structure of diamond

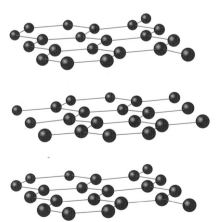

Graphite

The giant structure of graphite. When you write with a pencil, some layers of carbon atoms slide off the 'lead' and are left on the paper.

Higher

AQA *Examiner's tip*

Diamond and graphite both have very high melting points because they are both giant covalent structures.

Bump up your grade

If you are taking the higher paper, you should be able to explain the differences in the properties of graphite and diamond in terms of intermolecular forces and delocalised electrons.

Key words: giant covalent structure, macromolecule, fullerene

Student Book
pages 130–131 **C2**

2.4 Giant metallic structures

- Metal atoms are arranged in layers. When a force is applied the layers of atoms can slide over each other. They can move into a new position without breaking apart, so the metal bends or stretches into a new shape. This means that metals are useful for making wires, rods and sheet materials.

▶ **1** *Why can metals be made into wires?*

- Alloys are mixtures of metals or metals mixed with other elements. The different sized atoms in the mixture distort the layers in the metal structure and make it more difficult for them to slide over each other. This makes alloys harder than pure metals.
- **Shape memory alloys** can be bent or deformed into a different shape. When they are heated they return to their original shape. They can be used in many ways, for example as dental braces.

▶ **2** *Give two reasons why alloys can be more useful than pure metals.*

Metal structures

Metal structures have delocalised electrons. Metals are good conductors of heat and electricity because the delocalised electrons move throughout the giant metallic lattice and can transfer energy quickly.

▶ **3** *Why are metals good conductors of electricity?*

Key word: shape memory alloy

Key points

- When we bend and shape metals the layers of atoms in the giant metallic structure slide over each other.
- Alloys are mixtures of metals and are harder than pure metals because the layers in the structure are distorted.
- If a shape-memory alloy is deformed, it can return to its original shape on heating.
- Delocalised electrons in metals enable metals to conduct heat and electricity well. **[H]**

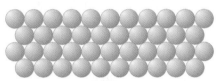

Iron

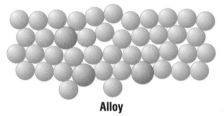

Alloy

The atoms in pure iron are arranged in layers that can easily slide over each other. In alloys the layers cannot slide so easily because atoms of other elements change the regular structure.

Student Book
pages 132–133 **C2**

2.5 The properties of polymers

- The properties of a polymer depend on the monomers used to make it, and the conditions we use to carry out the reaction. Poly(propene) is made from propene and softens at a higher temperature than poly(ethene), which is made from ethene. Low density (LD) poly(ethene) and high density (HD) poly(ethene) are made using different catalysts and different reaction conditions. HD poly(ethene) has a higher softening temperature and is stronger than LD poly(ethene).

▶ **1** *Why do LD and HD poly(ethene) have different properties?*

- Poly(ethene) is an example of a **thermosoftening polymer**. It is made up of individual polymer chains that are tangled together. When it is heated it becomes soft and hardens again when it cools. This means it can be heated to mould it into shape and it can be remoulded by heating it again.
- Other polymers called **thermosetting polymers** do not melt or soften when we heat them. These polymers set hard when they are first moulded because strong covalent bonds form cross-links between their polymer chains. The strong bonds hold the polymer chains in position.

Key points

- The properties of polymers depend on the monomers used to make them.
- Changing reaction conditions can also change the properties of the polymer that is produced.
- Thermosoftening polymers soften or melt easily when heated.
- Thermosetting polymers do not soften or melt when heated.

The strands of spaghetti are like the polymer molecules of a themosoftening polymer

Electrical sockets are made of thermosetting plastics

⫸ **2** *What is the main difference in the structures of thermosoftening and thermosetting polymers?*

Bonding in polymers

In thermosoftening polymers the forces between the polymer chains are weak. When we heat the polymer, these weak intermolecular forces are broken and the polymer becomes soft. When the polymer cools down, the intermolecular forces bring the polymer molecules back together so the polymer hardens again.

⫸ **3** *What allows thermosoftening polymers to be remoulded?*

AQA Examiner's tip

You should be able to recognise the type of polymer from a diagram of its structure or a description of its properties. Thermosetting polymers have covalent bonds linking the chains and do not soften when heated.

Key words: thermosoftening polymer, thermosetting polymer

Student Book
pages 134–135

C2

2.6 Nanoscience

Key points

- Nanoscience is the study of small particles that are between 1 and 100 nanometres in size.

- Nanoparticles behave differently from the bulk materials they are made from.

- Developments in nanoscience are exciting but will need more research into possible issues that might arise from increased use.

- **Nanoscience** is a new and exciting area of science. When atoms are arranged into very small particles they behave differently to ordinary materials made of the same atoms. A nanometre is one billionth of a metre (or 10^{-9} m) and nanoparticles are a few nanometres in size. They contain a few hundred atoms arranged in a particular way. Their very small sizes give them very large surface areas and new properties that can make them very useful materials.

⫸ **1** *What is a nanoparticle?*

- Nanotechnology uses nanoparticles as highly selective sensors, very efficient catalysts, new coatings, new cosmetics such as sun screens and deodorants, and to give construction materials special properties.

- If nanoparticles are used more and more there will be a greater risk of them finding their way into the air and into our bodies. This could have unpredictable consequences for our health and the environment. More research needs to be done to find out their effects.

⫸ **2** *Scientists have developed a new deodorant containing nanoparticles. What should be done before it is sold for people to use?*

Key word: nanoscience

Nanocages can carry drugs inside them

1 Why does it take a lot of energy to melt sodium chloride?

2 Why are compounds like methane, CH_4, and ammonia, NH_3, gases at room temperature?

3 Polymers made from different monomers have different properties. Explain why.

4 Some dental braces are made from shape-memory alloys. What is meant by a 'shape-memory alloy'?

5 Explain why diamonds are very hard.

6 Why do ionic compounds need to be molten or in solution to conduct electricity?

7 Explain why a block of copper can be hammered into a sheet.

8 Silver nanoparticles are used in some socks to help prevent bad smells.

    a How are silver nanoparticles different from ordinary silver particles?

    b Suggest why a sock manufacturer would use nanoparticles instead of ordinary silver particles.

9 Explain why thermosetting polymers are often used to make handles for cooking pans.

10 Explain how the atoms in a metal are bonded to each other. [H]

11 Why can graphite conduct electricity? [H]

12 Explain what is meant by 'intermolecular forces'. [H]

13 C_{60} is a fullerene. What are fullerenes? [H]

Chapter checklist	✓	✓	✓
Tick when you have:			
reviewed it after your lesson	✓	☐	☐
revised once – some questions right	✓	✓	☐
revised twice – all questions right	✓	✓	✓
Move on to another topic when you have all three ticks			

Giant ionic structures	☐	☐	☐
Simple molecules	☐	☐	☐
Giant covalent structures	☐	☐	☐
Giant metallic structures	☐	☐	☐
The properties of polymers	☐	☐	☐
Nanoscience	☐	☐	☐

3.1 The mass of atoms

- Protons and neutrons have the same mass and so the relative masses of a proton and a neutron are both one.
- The mass of an electron is very small compared with a proton or neutron, and so the mass of an atom is made up almost entirely of its protons and neutrons. The total number of protons and neutrons in an atom is called its **mass number**.

> **1** *Why do we count only protons and neutrons to calculate the mass number of an atom?*

- Atoms of the same element all have the same **atomic number**. The number of protons and electrons in an atom must always be the same, but there can be different numbers of neutrons.
- Atoms of the same element with different numbers of neutrons are called **isotopes**.
- The number of neutrons in an atom is equal to its mass number minus its atomic number. We can show the mass number and atomic number of an atom like this:

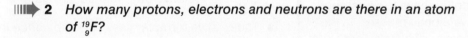

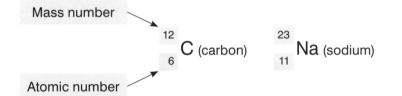

$^{12}_{6}$C (carbon) $^{23}_{11}$Na (sodium)

- The number at the top is the mass number (which is larger than the atomic number, except for hydrogen, $^{1}_{1}$H).
- So this sodium atom sodium has 11 protons, 11 electrons and (23 – 11 =) 12 neutrons.

> **2** *How many protons, electrons and neutrons are there in an atom of $^{19}_{9}$F?*

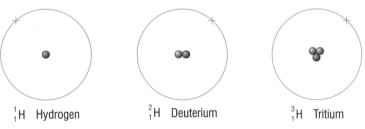

$^{1}_{1}$H Hydrogen $^{2}_{1}$H Deuterium $^{3}_{1}$H Tritium

The isotopes of hydrogen – they have identical chemical properties but different physical properties

> **3** *What are isotopes?*

Key words: mass number, atomic number, isotope

Key points

- The relative mass of protons and neutrons is 1.
- The atomic number of an atom is its number of protons (which equals its number of electrons).
- The mass number of an atom is the total number of protons and neutrons in its nucleus.
- Isotopes are atoms of the same element with different numbers of neutrons.

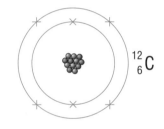

● Proton	Number of protons gives atomic number
● Neutron	Number of protons plus number of neutrons gives mass number

An atom of carbon

AQA *Examiner's tip*

Isotopes are atoms of the same element. They have the same chemical properties but they have different physical properties because of their different masses. Some isotopes are unstable and radioactive.

C2

3.2 Masses of atoms and moles

Key points

- We use relative atomic masses to compare the masses of atoms.

- The relative atomic mass of an element is an average value for the isotopes of an element. **[H]**

- We work out the relative formula mass of a compound by adding up the relative atomic masses of the elements in it.

- One mole of any substance is its relative formula mass in grams.

Bump up your grade

Make sure you can calculate the relative formula mass (M_r) of a compound from its formula.

AQA Examiner's tip

You do not have to remember relative atomic masses. In the exam you will have a data sheet with a periodic table that shows the relative atomic mass of each element.

- Atoms are much too small to weigh and so we use **relative atomic masses (A_r)** in calculations. Relative atomic masses are often shown in periodic tables. In the laboratory we usually weigh substances in grams. The relative atomic mass of an element in grams is called one **mole** of atoms of the element.

▶ **1** *What is the mass of one mole of sodium atoms?*

Relative atomic mass

We use an atom of $^{12}_{6}C$ as a standard atom and compare the masses of all other atoms with this. The relative atomic mass of an element (A_r) is an average value that depends on the isotopes the element contains. However, when rounded to a whole number it is often the same as the mass number of the main isotope of the element.

▶ **2** *Why is the relative atomic mass of chlorine not a whole number?*

- The **relative formula mass (M_r)** of a substance is found by adding up the relative atomic masses of the atoms in its formula.

Maths skills

Worked example	Answer
Calculate the M_r of calcium chloride, $CaCl_2$	A_r of Ca = 40, A_r of Cl = 35.5, so M_r = 40 + (35.5 × 2) = 111

▶ **3** *Calculate the relative formula mass (M_r) of sodium sulfate, Na_2SO_4. (Relative atomic masses: Na = 23, S = 32, O = 16).*

- The relative formula mass of a substance in grams is called one mole of that substance. Using moles of substances is useful when we need to work out how much of a substance reacts or how much product we will get.

Maths skills

Worked example	Answer
What is the mass of one mole of sodium hydroxide, NaOH?	A_r of Na = 23, A_r of O = 16, A_r of H = 1, so 1 mole NaOH = (23 + 16 + 1) g = 40 g

▶ **4** *What is the mass of one mole of magnesium carbonate, $MgCO_3$? (Relative atomic masses: Mg = 24, C = 12, O = 16).*

Key words: relative atomic mass, mole, relative formula mass

3.3 Percentages and formulae

- We can calculate the percentage of any of the elements in a compound from the formula of the compound. Divide the relative atomic mass of the element by the relative formula mass of the compound and multiply the answer by 100 to convert it to a percentage. This can be useful when deciding if a compound is suitable for a particular purpose or to identify a compound.

Key points

- The relative atomic masses of the elements in a compound and its formula can be used to work out its percentage composition.

- We can calculate empirical formulae given the masses or percentage composition of elements present. **[H]**

Maths skills

Worked example

What is the percentage of carbon in carbon dioxide, CO_2?

Answer

A_r of C = 12, A_r of O = 16

M_r of CO_2 = 12 + (16 × 2) = 44

So percentage of carbon

= (12/44) × 100 = 27.3%

AQA Examiner's tip

When calculating an empirical formula it is helpful to set out your answer in a table. In the exam you should always show your working in calculations.

▶ **1** *What is the percentage of carbon in methane, CH_4? (A_r of C = 12, A_r of H = 1).*

Working out the formula of a compound from its percentage composition

The **empirical formula** is the simplest ratio of the atoms or ions in a compound. It is the formula used for ionic compounds, but for covalent compounds it is not always the same as the **molecular formula**. For example, the molecular formula of ethane is C_2H_6, but its empirical formula is CH_3.

We can calculate the empirical formula of a compound from its percentage composition:

- Divide the mass of each element in 100 g of the compound by its A_r to give the ratio of atoms.

- Then convert this to the simplest whole number ratio.

Bump up your grade

Practice calculating the percentage of an element in a compound from its formula.

If you are taking the Higher Tier paper you should be able to calculate the empirical formula of a compound with two or three elements from information about its percentage composition.

Maths skills

Worked example

What is the empirical formula of the hydrocarbon that contains 80% carbon?

Answer:

	Carbon	Hydrogen
Mass in 100 g of compound	80	20
Ratio of atoms or moles of atoms (mass/A_r)	80/12 = 6.67	20/1 = 20
Simplest ratio of atoms (divide by smallest)	6.67/6.67 = 1	20/6.67 = 3
Empirical formula	CH_3	

A small difference in the amount of metal in an ore might not seem very much. However, when millions of tonnes of ore are extracted and processed each year, it all adds up!

▶ **2** *What is the empirical formula of the compound that contains 70% iron and 30% oxygen? (A_r of Fe = 56, A_r of O = 16)*

Key words: empirical formula, molecular formula

Higher

3.4 Equations and calculations

Key points

- Balanced symbol equations tell us the number of moles of substances involved in a chemical reaction. **[H]**

- We can use balanced symbol equations to calculate the masses of reactants and products in a chemical reaction. **[H]**

AQA Examiner's tip

You can work in moles or you can use relative masses when doing calculations, but if you are asked to calculate a mass of a reactant or product do not forget to give the correct units in your answer.

Calculating masses from chemical equations

Chemical equations show the reactants and products of a reaction. When they are balanced they show the amounts of atoms, molecules or ions in the reaction. For example: $2Mg + O_2 \rightarrow 2MgO$ shows that two atoms of magnesium react with one molecule of oxygen to form two magnesium ions and two oxide ions.

If we work in moles, the equation tells us that two moles of magnesium atoms react with one mole of oxygen molecules to produce two moles of magnesium oxide.

This means that 48 g of magnesium react with 32 g of oxygen to give 80 g of magnesium oxide. (A_r of Mg = 24, A_r of O = 16)

Alternatively, if we work in relative masses from the equation: $(2 \times A_r$ of Mg$) + (2 \times A_r$ of O) gives $(2 \times M_r$ of MgO)

Converting this to grams it becomes 2×24 g Mg + 2×16 g O gives 2×40 g MgO or 48 g Mg + 32 g O gives 80 g MgO (which is the same as when we used moles).

If we have 5 g of magnesium, we can work out the mass of magnesium oxide it will produce using ratios: 1 g Mg will produce 80/48 g MgO

so 5 g Mg will produce $5 \times 80/48$ g MgO = 8.33 g of MgO

If we use moles the calculation can be done like this:

1 mole of Mg produces 1 mole of MgO

5 g Mg = 5/24 mole of magnesium and so it will produce 5/24 mole of MgO.

The mass of 5/24 mole MgO = $5/24 \times 40$ g = 8.33 g of MgO

> **1** Calculate the mass of calcium oxide that can be made from 10 g of calcium carbonate in the reaction:
> $CaCO_3 \rightarrow CaO + CO_2$ (A_r of Ca = 40, A_r of O = 16, A_r of C = 12)

3.5 The yield of a chemical reaction

Key points

- The yield of a chemical reaction describes how much product is made.

- The percentage yield of a chemical reaction tells us how much product is made compared with the maximum amount that could be made.

- It is important to maximise yield and minimise energy wasted to conserve the Earth's limited resources and reduce pollution.

- The **yield** of a chemical process is how much you actually make. The **percentage yield** compares the amount made with the maximum amount that could be made, calculated as a percentage.

Calculating percentage yield

The percentage yield is calculated using this equation:

$$\text{Percentage yield} = \frac{\text{(amount of product collected}}{\text{maximum amount of product possible)}} \times 100\%$$

The maximum amount of product possible is calculated from the balanced equation for the reaction.

For example: A student collected 2.3 g of magnesium oxide from 2.0 g of magnesium.

Theoretically: $2Mg + O_2 \rightarrow 2MgO$, so 48 g of Mg should give 80 g of MgO, and so 2.0 g of Mg should give $2 \times 80/48 = 3.33$ g of MgO.

$$\text{Percentage yield} = \left(\frac{2.3}{3.33}\right) \times 100 = 69\%$$

All students should understand the idea of percentage yield but only Higher Tier candidates will be expected to calculate percentage yields.

Bump up your grade

If you are taking the Higher Tier paper you should be able to calculate the percentage yield of a reaction from information about the mass of product obtained and the equation for the reaction.

▥➡ **1** *A student made 4.4 g of calcium oxide from 4.0 g of calcium. Calculate the percentage yield.* **[H]**

● When you actually do chemical reactions it is not usually possible to collect the amounts calculated from the chemical equations. Reactions may not go to completion, other reactions may happen and some product may be lost when it is separated or collected from the apparatus.

▥➡ **2** *Why is it not usually possible to get 100% yield from a chemical reaction?*

● Using reactions with high yields in industry helps to conserve resources and to reduce waste. Chemical processes should also waste as little energy as possible. Working in these ways helps to reduce pollution and makes production more sustainable.

▥➡ **3** *Why should chemical manufacturers use reactions with high yields?*

Key words: yield, percentage yield

Student Book
pages 148–149 **C2**

3.6 Reversible reactions

Key points

● In a reversible reaction the products of the reaction can react to make the original reactants.

● We can show a reversible reaction using the (reversible reaction) sign ⇌.

● If the products of a chemical reaction can react to produce the reactants, the reaction can go in both directions. This type of reaction is called a **reversible reaction** and is represented with the symbol ⇌. One arrow points in the forwards direction (to the right) and one backwards.

● An example of a reversible reaction is:

ammonium chloride ⇌ ammonia + hydrogen chloride

● When heated, ammonium chloride decomposes to produce ammonia and hydrogen chloride. When cooled, ammonia and hydrogen chloride react to produce ammonium chloride.

▥➡ **1** *What is a reversible reaction?*

You should know that the thermal decomposition of ammonium chloride is just one example of a reversible reaction and that there are many others. You do not have to remember any other examples but may be given information about other reversible reactions in the exam.

Key word: reversible reaction

Heating ammonium chloride: an example of a reversible reaction

Student Book
pages 150–151 **C2**

3.7 Analysing substances

- Substances added to food to improve its qualities are called food additives. Food additives may be natural products or synthetic chemicals.

Key points

- Chemical analysis is used to identify food additives.
- Paper chromatography can be used to detect and identify artificial colours.

- Foods can be checked by chemical analysis to ensure only safe, permitted additives have been used. The methods used include paper **chromatography** and mass spectrometry.
- Paper chromatography can be used to analyse the artificial colours in food. A spot of colour is put onto paper and a solvent is allowed to move through the paper. The colours move different distances depending on their solubility.

1 *What method can be used to analyse the colours in food?*

Key word: chromatography

AQA Examiner's tip

You do not need to remember the names of specific food additives or what they are used for.

Student Book
pages 152–153 **C2**

3.8 Instrumental analysis

Key points

- Modern instrumental techniques provide fast, accurate and sensitive ways of analysing chemical substances.
- Compounds in a mixture can be separated using gas chromatography.
- Once separated, compounds can be identified using a mass spectrometer.
- The mass spectrometer can be used to find the relative molecular mass of a compound from its molecular ion peak. **[H]**

- Modern instrumental methods of analysis are rapid, accurate and sensitive, often using very small samples. Computers process the data from the instrument to give meaningful results almost instantly. The equipment is usually very expensive and special training is needed to use it.
- Samples for analysis are often mixtures that need to be separated so that the compounds can be identified. One way of doing this is to use **gas chromatography** linked to a **mass spectrometer**.
- In gas chromatography the mixture is carried by a gas through a long column packed with particles of a solid. The individual compounds travel at different speeds through the column and come out at different times. The amount of substance leaving the column at different times is recorded against time and shows the number of compounds in the mixture and their retention times. The **retention times** can be compared with the results for known compounds to help identify the compounds in the mixture.
- The output from the gas chromatography column can be linked directly to a mass spectrometer (GC–MS). The mass spectrometer gives further data that a computer can use quickly to identify the individual compounds.

1 *What is the main purpose of the gas chromatography column in GC–MS analysis?*

Measuring relative molecular masses

A mass spectrometer can give the relative molecular mass of a compound. For an individual compound the peak with the largest mass corresponds to an ion with just one electron removed. This peak is called the **molecular ion peak** and is furthest to the right on a mass spectrum.

2 *How is the relative molecular mass shown in a mass spectrum?*

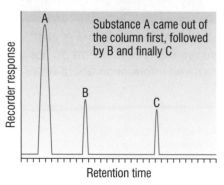

Substance A came out of the column first, followed by B and finally C

This is a gas chromatogram of a mixture of three different compounds

Key words: gas chromatography, mass spectrometer, retention time, molecular ion peak

1 There are two main types of chlorine atom, $^{35}_{17}Cl$ and $^{37}_{17}Cl$.

  a What name is used for these two types of atom?

  b How is an atom of $^{35}_{17}Cl$ different from an atom of $^{37}_{17}Cl$?

2 Hydrogen and iodine react to make hydrogen iodide. The equation for the reaction is:

$$H_2 + I_2 \rightleftharpoons 2HI$$

What type of reaction is this?

3 What substances in foods can be detected by paper chromatography?

4 What is the relative formula mass of magnesium fluoride, MgF_2?

5 What is the mass of one mole of aluminium oxide, Al_2O_3?

6 What is the percentage by mass of copper in copper(ii) carbonate, $CuCO_3$?

7 A student made some magnesium oxide by burning magnesium in air. The student obtained a yield of 55%. Suggest two reasons why the yield was less than 100%.

8 What is the empirical formula of vanadium oxide that contains 56% of vanadium?   [H]

9 Calculate the mass of zinc chloride that you can make from 6.5 g of zinc.

$$Zn + 2HCl \rightarrow ZnCl_2 + H_2$$ [H]

10 Calculate the percentage yield if 9.0 g $MgSO_4$ was made from 4.0 g MgO.   [H]

11 What information can be obtained from the molecular ion peak in a mass spectrum?   [H]

Chapter checklist	✓ ✓ ✓

Tick when you have:				The mass of atoms	☐ ☐ ☐
reviewed it after your lesson	✓	☐	☐	Masses of atoms and moles	☐ ☐ ☐
revised once – some questions right	✓	✓	☐	Percentages and formulae	☐ ☐ ☐
revised twice – all questions right	✓	✓	✓	Equations and calculations	☐ ☐ ☐
Move on to another topic when you have all three ticks				The yield of a chemical reaction	☐ ☐ ☐
				Reversible reactions	☐ ☐ ☐
				Analysing substances	☐ ☐ ☐
				Instrumental analysis	☐ ☐ ☐

Student Book
pages 156–157
C2

4.1 How fast?

- The **rate** of a reaction measures the speed of a reaction or how fast it is. The rate can be found by measuring how much of a reactant is used, or how much of a product is formed, and the time taken.
- Alternatively the rate can be found by measuring the time taken for a certain amount of reactant to be used or product to be formed. These methods give the average rate for the time measured.

$$\text{Rate of reaction} = \frac{\text{amount of reactant used}}{\text{time}} \quad \text{OR} \quad \frac{\text{amount of product formed}}{\text{time}}$$

- An average rate can also be found by measuring the time it takes for a certain amount of solid to appear in a solution. If a gas is given off in the reaction, its average rate can be found by measuring the time taken to collect a certain amount of gas.

▶ **1** *What two types of measurement must be made to find the average rate of a reaction?*

- The rate of a reaction at any given time can be found from the **gradient,** or slope, of the line on a graph of amount of reactant or product against time. The steeper the gradient is, the faster the reaction is at that time.
- A graph can be produced by measuring the mass of gas released or the volume of gas produced at intervals of time. Other possible ways include measuring changes in the colour, concentration, or pH of a reaction mixture over time.

▶ **2** *How can we use a graph of amount of product against time to tell us the rate of the reaction at a given time?*

Key word: gradient

Key points

- We can find the rate of a chemical reaction by measuring the amount of reactants used up over time or by measuring the amount of products made over time.
- The gradient or slope of the line on a graph of amount of reactant or product against time tells us the rate of reaction at that time. The steeper the gradient, the faster the reaction.

AQA Examiner's tip

The faster the rate, the shorter the time it takes for the reaction to finish. So rate is inversely proportional to time.

Student Book
pages 158–159
C2

4.2 Collision theory and surface area

- The **collision theory** states that reactions can only happen if particles collide. However, just colliding is not enough. The particles must collide with enough energy to change into new substances. The minimum energy they need to react is called the **activation energy**.

▶ **1** *What do we call the minimum energy needed for particles to react?*

- Factors that increase the chance of collisions, or the energy of the particles, will increase the rate of the reaction.
  Increasing the:
  - temperature,
  - concentration of solutions,
  - pressure of gases,
  - surface area of solids, and
  - using a catalyst
  will increase the rate of a reaction.

▶ **2** *List the factors that increase the rate of a reaction.*

Key points

- Particles must collide with a certain amount of energy before they can react.
- The minimum amount of energy that particles must have in order to react is called the activation energy.
- The rate of a chemical reaction increases if the surface area of any solid reactants is increased. This increases the frequency of collisions between reacting particles.

AQA *Examiner's tip*

Increasing the surface area means making the pieces smaller. More surface area produces more frequent collisions and so the rate of reaction is faster with powders than with larger pieces of solid.

● Breaking large pieces of a solid into smaller pieces exposes new surfaces and so increases the surface area. This means there are more collisions in the same time. So a powder reacts faster than large lumps of a substance. The finer the powder the faster the reaction.

3 Why do powders react faster than large pieces of solid?

Bump up your grade

Be careful with your use of language: increasing the surface area of a solid increases the frequency of the collisions. This means there are more collisions in the same time and this increases the rate of reaction. It is not enough to just write 'more collisions'.

Key words: collision theory, activation energy

Student Book
pages 160–161 **C2**

4.3 The effect of temperature

Key points

● Reactions happen more quickly as the temperature increases.

● Increasing the temperature increases the rate of reaction because particles collide more frequently and more energetically.

● At a higher temperature more of the collisions result in a reaction because a higher proportion of particles have energy greater than the activation energy.

● Increasing the temperature increases the speed of the particles in a reaction mixture. This means they collide more often, which increases the rate of reaction. As well as colliding more frequently they collide with more energy, which also increases the rate of reaction.

● Therefore, a small change in temperature has a large effect on reaction rates. At ordinary temperatures a rise of 10 °C will roughly double the rate of many reactions, so they go twice as fast. A decrease in temperature will slow reactions down, and a decrease of 10 °C will double the time that many reactions take. This is why we refrigerate or freeze food so it stays fresh for longer.

1 Why does a small change in temperature have a large effect on the rate of reaction?

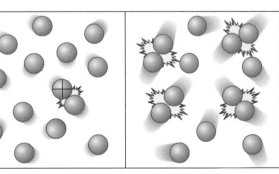

Cold –
slow movement,
less frequent
collisions,
little energy

Hot –
fast movement,
more frequent
collisions,
more energy

More frequent collisions, with more energy – both of these factors increase the rate of a chemical reaction caused by increasing the temperature.

AQA *Examiner's tip*

Increasing the temperature has a large effect on the rate of a reaction because it increases the frequency of collisions and it increases the energy of the particles.

Bump up your grade

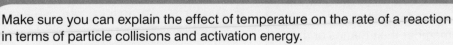

Make sure you can explain the effect of temperature on the rate of a reaction in terms of particle collisions and activation energy.

Student Book
pages 162–163 **C2**

4.4 The effect of concentration or pressure

Key points

- Increasing the concentration of reactants in solutions increases the frequency of collisions between particles, and so increases the rate of reaction.

- Increasing the pressure of reacting gases also increases the frequency of collisions and so increases the rate of reaction.

Bump up your grade

Make sure you can explain the effect of concentration on the rate of a reaction in terms of particle collisions. You should also be able to explain the effect of pressure on reactions of gases.

- The particles in a solution are moving around randomly. If the concentration of a solution is increased there are more particles dissolved in the same volume. This means the dissolved particles are closer together and so they collide more often.

- Increasing the concentration of a reactant therefore increases the rate of a reaction because the particles collide more frequently.

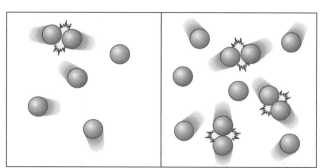

Increasing concentration and pressure mean that particles are closer together. This increases the frequency of collisions between particles, so the reaction rate increases.

▷▷▷ **1** *Why do reactions in solutions go faster at higher concentrations?*

- In a similar way, increasing the pressure of a gas puts more molecules into the same volume, and so they collide more frequently. This increases the rate of reactions that have gases as reactants.

▷▷▷ **2** *Why does increasing the pressure increase the rate of a reaction of two gases?*

Student Book
pages 164–165 **C2**

4.5 The effect of catalysts

Key points

- A catalyst speeds up the rate of a chemical reaction.

- A catalyst is not used up during a chemical reaction.

- Different catalysts are needed for different reactions.

AQA Examiner's tip

You may have studied some specific examples of catalysts but you do not need to remember their names or the reactions they catalyse.

- **Catalysts** change the rates of chemical reactions. Most catalysts are used to speed up reactions. Catalysts that speed up reactions lower the activation energy of the reaction so that more of the collisions result in a reaction.

- Although the catalyst changes the rate of the reaction it is not used up. The catalyst is left at the end of the reaction and so it can be used over and over again.

▷▷▷ **1** *Why can catalysts be used over and over again?*

- Catalysts that are solids are used in forms that have large surface areas to make them as effective as possible.

- Catalysts often work with only one type of reaction and so different reactions need different catalysts.

▷▷▷ **2** *Why do different reactions need different catalysts?*

Key word: catalyst

Student Book
pages 166–167

C2

4.6 Catalysts in action ⚙️

- Some catalysts are expensive but they can be economical because they do not need replacing very often. They are used in many industrial processes because they can reduce the energy and the time needed for reactions. This helps to reduce costs and reduce impacts on the environment. If fossil fuels are burned to provide energy for industrial reactions, using catalysts will help to conserve resources and reduce pollution.

▶ **1** *What are the benefits of using catalysts in industrial processes?*

- Many of the catalysts used in industry involve transition metals and their compounds. Some of these metals and their compounds are toxic and may cause harm if they get into the environment.

▶ **2** *Give one disadvantage of transition metal catalysts.*

- Finding new and better catalysts is a major area of research for the chemical industry. Nanoparticles offer exciting possibilities for developing new, highly efficient catalysts. Enzymes are biological catalysts that work at ordinary temperatures. If they can replace more traditional catalysts they will reduce energy costs even further.

▶ **3** *What two areas of research offer possibilities for new or better catalysts?*

Key points

- Catalysts are used in industry to increase the rate of reactions and reduce energy costs.
- Traditional catalysts are often transition metals or their compounds.
- Modern catalysts are being developed in industry which result in less waste and are safer for the environment.

AQA Examiner's tip

You should be aware of some of the issues involved in the use of catalysts but you do not need to remember the names of any specific examples.

Student Book
pages 168–169

C2

4.7 Exothermic and endothermic reactions

- When chemical reactions take place energy is transferred as bonds are broken and made. Reactions that transfer energy to the surroundings are called **exothermic** reactions. The energy transferred often heats up the surroundings and so the temperature increases.

Exothermic reactions include:
- combustion, such as burning fuels,
- oxidation reactions, such as respiration, and
- neutralisation reactions involving acids and bases.

▶ **1** *How can you tell that burning natural gas is an exothermic reaction?*

- **Endothermic** reactions take in energy from the surroundings.
- Some cause a decrease in temperature and others require a supply of energy. When some solid compounds are mixed with water, the temperature decreases because endothermic changes happen as they dissolve.
- **Thermal decomposition** reactions need to be heated continuously to keep the reaction going.

▶ **2** *What are the two ways that show that a reaction is endothermic?*

Key words: exothermic, endothermic, thermal decomposition

Key points

- Energy may be transferred to or from the reacting substances in a reaction.
- A reaction in which energy is transferred from the reacting substances to their surroundings is called an exothermic reaction.
- A reaction in which energy is transferred to the reacting substances from their surroundings is called an endothermic reaction.

Bump up your grade

Make sure you can recognise a reaction as exothermic or endothermic from temperature changes provided.

Student Book
pages 170–171 **C2**

4.8 Energy and reversible reactions

Key points

- In reversible reactions, the reaction in one direction is exothermic and in the other direction it is endothermic.

- In any reversible reaction, the amount of energy released when the reaction goes in one direction is exactly equal to the energy absorbed when the reaction goes in the opposite direction.

- In reversible reactions, the forward and reverse reactions involve equal but opposite energy transfers. A reversible reaction that is exothermic in one direction must be endothermic in the other direction. The amount of energy released by the exothermic reaction exactly equals the amount taken in by the endothermic reaction.

- When blue copper sulfate crystals are heated the reaction is endothermic:

$$\underset{\substack{\textbf{hydrated}\\\text{copper sulfate}}}{\underset{\text{blue crystals}}{CuSO_4 \cdot 5H_2O}} \rightleftharpoons \underset{\substack{\textbf{anhydrous}\\\text{copper sulfate}}}{\underset{\text{white powder}}{CuSO_4}} + 5H_2O$$

▐▶ **1** *Why must blue copper sulfate be heated continuously to change it into anhydrous copper sulfate?*

- When water is added to anhydrous copper sulfate the reaction is exothermic.

▐▶ **2** *Why does adding water to anhydrous copper sulfate cause the mixture to get hot?*

Key words: hydrated, anhydrous

Student Book
pages 172–173 **C2**

4.9 Using energy transfers from reactions

Key points

- Exothermic changes can be used in hand warmers and self-heating cans.

- Endothermic changes can be used in instant cold packs for sports injuries.

- Exothermic reactions can be used to heat things. Hand warmers and self-heating cans use exothermic reactions. In some hand warmers and cans the reactants are used up and so they cannot be used again. They use reactions such as the oxidation of iron or the reaction of calcium oxide with water. Other hand warmers use a reversible reaction such as the crystallisation of a salt. Once used, the pack can be heated in boiling water to re-dissolve the salt. These can be re-used many times.

▐▶ **1** *Suggest one advantage and one disadvantage of a re-usable hand warmer compared with a single use hand warmer.*

- Endothermic changes can be used to cool things. Some chemical cold packs contain ammonium nitrate and water that are kept separated. When mixed together the ammonium nitrate dissolves and takes in energy from the surroundings. The cold pack can be used on sports injuries or to cool drinks. The reaction is reversible but not in the pack and so this type of pack can be used only once.

▐▶ **2** *Suggest one advantage and one disadvantage of a chemical cold pack compared with using an ice pack.*

A reusable hand warmer based on recrystallisation

Instant cold packs can be applied to injuries

AQA *Examiner's tip*

You should know some examples of types of application of exothermic and endothermic reactions such as hand warmers and cold packs, but you do not need to remember the details of how they work or the reactions that are used. However, you may be asked to evaluate information that you are given about specific applications.

1 Pieces of zinc react with dilute hydrochloric acid:

$$Zn(s) + 2HCl(aq) \rightarrow ZnCl_2(aq) + H_2(g)$$

In what ways could you increase the rate of the reaction between zinc and hydrochloric acid?

2 How can you find the rate of a reaction from a graph of mass of product against time?

3 What is meant by the 'activation energy' of a reaction?

4 Name two types of reaction that are exothermic.

5 Why must calcium carbonate be heated continuously to convert it into calcium oxide and carbon dioxide?

6 Nitrogen and oxygen react together to produce nitrogen oxide:

$$N_2(g) + O_2(g) \rightarrow 2NO(g)$$

What changes in conditions would increase the rate of this reaction?

7 Explain in terms of particles why increasing the concentration of a reactant increases the rate of the reaction.

8 Explain why increasing the temperature increases the rate of a reaction.

Chapter checklist ✔ ✔ ✔

Tick when you have:				How fast?	☐	☐	☐
reviewed it after your lesson	✔	☐	☐	Collision theory and surface area	☐	☐	☐
revised once – some questions right	✔	✔	☐	The effect of temperature	☐	☐	☐
revised twice – all questions right	✔	✔	✔	The effect of concentration or pressure	☐	☐	☐
Move on to another topic when you have all three ticks				The effect of catalysts	☐	☐	☐
				Catalysts in action	☐	☐	☐
				Exothermic and endothermic reactions	☐	☐	☐
				Energy and reversible reactions	☐	☐	☐
				Using energy transfers from reactions	☐	☐	☐

Student Book
pages 176–177

C2

5.1 Acids and alkalis

Key points

- When acids are added to water they produce hydrogen ions, $H^+(aq)$, in the solution.
- Bases are substances that will neutralise acids.
- Alkalis dissolve in water to give hydroxide ions, $OH^-(aq)$, in the solution.
- The pH scale shows how acidic or alkaline a solution is.

AQA *Examiner's tip*

All alkalis are bases, and all bases neutralise acids, but only bases that dissolve in water are alkalis.

- Pure water is **neutral** and has a pH value of 7.
- **Acids** are substances that produce hydrogen ions, $H^+(aq)$, when they are added to water.
- When we dissolve a substance in water we make an **aqueous solution**.
- The **state symbol** (aq) shows that the ions are in aqueous solution. Hydrogen ions make solutions acidic and they have pH values of less than 7.

▶ **1** *Which ions are produced by acids when they are added to water?*

- **Bases** react with acids and neutralise them.
- **Alkalis** are bases that dissolve in water to make alkaline solutions. Alkalis produce hydroxide ions, $OH^-(aq)$, in the solution. Alkaline solutions have pH values greater than 7.

▶ **2** *What is an alkali?*

- The **pH scale** has values from 0 to 14. Solutions that are very acidic have low pH values of between 0 and 2. Solutions that are very alkaline have high pH values of 12 to 14.
- **Indicators** have different colours in acidic and alkaline solutions. **Universal indicator (UI)** and full-range indicators have different colours at different pH values.

▶ **3** *Which indicators can tell us the pH of a solution?*

Key words: neutral, acid, aqueous solution, state symbol, base, alkali, pH scale, universal indicator (UI)

Student Book
pages 178–179

C2

5.2 Making salts from metals or bases

Key points

- When an acid reacts with a base a neutralisation reaction takes place and produces a salt and water.
- Some salts can be made by the reaction of a metal with an acid. This reaction produces hydrogen gas as well as a salt.
- Salts can be crystallised from solutions by evaporating off water.

- Acids will react with metals that are above hydrogen in the reactivity series.
- However, the reactions of acids with very reactive metals, such as sodium and potassium, are too violent to be done safely.
- When metals react with acids they produce a salt and hydrogen gas.

$$\text{acid} + \text{metal} \rightarrow \text{a salt} + \text{hydrogen}$$
$$H_2SO_4(aq) + Zn(s) \rightarrow ZnSO_4(aq) + H_2(g)$$

▶ **1** *Name a metal other than zinc that can safely react with an acid to produce a salt.*

- Metal oxides and metal hydroxides are bases. When an acid reacts with a base a **neutralisation** reaction takes place and a salt and water are produced.

$$\text{acid} + \text{base} \rightarrow \text{a salt} + \text{water}$$
$$2HCl(aq) + MgO(s) \rightarrow MgCl_2(aq) + H_2O(l)$$

AQA *Examiner's tip*

Learn the formulae of the three important acids HCl, HNO_3 and H_2SO_4 to help you to write the formulae of their salts. Remember that when they form salts hydrogen is lost from the acid so they form chlorides, nitrates and sulfates.

- These reactions can be used to make salts.
- A metal, or a base that is insoluble in water, is added a little at a time to the acid until all of the acid has reacted. The mixture is then filtered to remove the excess solid reactant, leaving a solution of the salt.
- The solid salt is made when water is evaporated from the solution so that it crystallises.

▐▐▐➡ **2** *Why do we add excess of the base when making a salt?*

- Chlorides are made from hydrochloric acid, nitrates from nitric acid and sulfates from sulfuric acid.

▐▐▐➡ **3** *Name the products when (a) nitric acid reacts with magnesium, (b) hydrochloric acid reacts with copper hydroxide.*

Key words: salt, neutralisation

Student Book
pages 180–181

C2

5.3 Making salts from solutions

Key points

- When a soluble salt is made from an alkali and an acid, an indicator can be used to show when the reaction is complete.
- Insoluble salts can be made by reacting two solutions to produce a precipitate.
- Precipitation is an important way of removing some metal ions from industrial waste water.

AQA *Examiner's tip*

You do not need to remember which salts are soluble or insoluble because you will be told about the solubility of salts in any exam questions.

- We can make soluble salts by reacting an acid and an alkali:

$$\text{acid} + \text{alkali} \rightarrow \text{salt} + \text{water}$$

e.g. $\text{HCl(aq)} + \text{NaOH(aq)} \rightarrow \text{NaCl(aq)} + H_2O(l)$

- We can represent the neutralisation reaction between any acid and any alkali by this equation:

$$H^+(aq) + OH^-(aq) \rightarrow H_2O(l)$$

- There is no visible change when acids react with alkalis so we need to use an indicator or a pH meter to show when the reaction is complete. The solid salt can be obtained from the solution by crystallisation.

▐▐▐➡ **1** *What compound is produced in every neutralisation reaction?*

- Ammonia solution is an alkali that does not contain a metal. It reacts with acids to produce ammonium salts, such as ammonium nitrate, NH_4NO_3. Ammonium salts are used as fertilisers.
- We can make insoluble salts by mixing solutions of soluble salts that contain the ions needed. For example, we can make lead iodide by mixing solutions of lead nitrate and potassium iodide. The lead iodide forms a **precipitate** that can be filtered from the solution, washed with distilled water and dried.

$$\text{Pb(NO}_3)_2\text{(aq)} + 2\text{KI(aq)} \rightarrow \text{PbI}_2\text{(s)} + 2\text{KNO}_3\text{(aq)}$$

- Some pollutants, such as metal ions, can be removed from water by **precipitation**. The water is treated by adding substances that react with the pollutant metal ions dissolved in the water to form insoluble salts.

▐▐▐➡ **2** *Zinc carbonate is insoluble in water. What would happen when sodium carbonate solution is added to zinc sulfate solution?*

Key word: precipitate

Student Book
pages 182–183 **C2**

5.4 Electrolysis

- Electrolysis is the process that uses electricity to break down ionic compounds into elements.
- When electricity is passed through a molten ionic compound or a solution containing ions, electrolysis takes place.
- The substance that is broken down is called the **electrolyte**.

IIIIII➡ 1 *What must be done to ionic compounds before they can be electrolysed?*

- The electrical circuit has two electrodes that make contact with the electrolyte. The electrodes are often made of an **inert** substance that does not react with the products.
- The ions in the electrolyte move to the electrodes where they are discharged to produce elements.
- Positively charged ions are attracted to the negative electrode where they form metals or hydrogen, depending on the ions in the electrolyte.
- Negatively charged ions are attracted to the positive electrode where they lose their charge to form non-metallic elements.

For example, when molten lead bromide is electrolysed, lead is produced at the negative electrode. At the same time bromine is produced at the positive electrode.

IIIIII➡ 2 *Molten zinc chloride is electrolysed. Name the substances produced (a) at the positive electrode and (b) at the negative electrode.*

Key words: electrolyte, inert

Key points

- Electrolysis splits up a substance using electricity.
- Ionic compounds can only be electrolysed when they are molten or in solution because then their ions are free to move to the electrodes.
- In electrolysis, positive ions move to the negative electrode and negative ions move to the positive electrode.

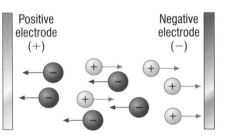

Positive electrode (+)   Negative electrode (−)

An ion always moves towards the oppositely charged electrode

Student Book
pages 184–185 **C2**

5.5 Changes at the electrodes

- When positively charged ions reach the negative electrode they gain electrons to become neutral atoms.
- Gaining electrons is called **reduction**, so the positive ions have been reduced. Ions with a single positive charge gain one electron and those with a 2+ charge gain 2 electrons.
- At the positive electrode, negative ions lose electrons to become neutral atoms. This is **oxidation**. Some non-metal atoms combine to form molecules, for example bromine forms Br_2.

IIIIII➡ 1 *What type of change happens at the negative electrode when sodium ions become sodium atoms?*

Half equations

We can represent the changes at the electrodes by half equations. The half equations for lead bromide are:

At the negative electrode: $Pb^{2+} + 2e^- \rightarrow Pb$

At the positive electrode: $2Br^- \rightarrow Br_2 + 2e^-$

IIIIII➡ 2 *Complete the half equation for the formation of chlorine at a positive electrode: $2Cl^- \rightarrow ... + ...$*

Key points

- Negative ions lose electrons and so are oxidised at the positive electrode.
- Positive ions gain electrons and so are reduced at the negative electrode.
- When aqueous solutions are electrolysed, oxygen gas is produced at the positive electrode unless the solution contains halide ions.
- When aqueous solutions are electrolysed, hydrogen gas is produced at the negative electrode unless the solution contains ions of a metal that is less reactive than hydrogen.

• Water contains hydrogen ions and hydroxide ions.

• When solutions of ions in water are electrolysed, hydrogen may be produced at the negative electrode. This happens if the other positive ions in the solution are those of a metal more reactive than hydrogen.

• At the positive electrode oxygen is usually produced from aqueous solutions. However, if the solution contains a reasonably high concentration of a halide ion, then a halogen will be produced.

▶ **3** *Name the products at (a) the positive and (b) the negative electrodes when aqueous copper sulfate solution is electrolysed using carbon electrodes.*

AQA Examiner's tip

Remember **OILRIG** –
Oxidation **I**s **L**oss (of electrons),
Reduction **I**s **G**ain (of electrons).

Key words: reduction, oxidation

5.6 The extraction of aluminium

Key points

• Aluminium oxide is electrolysed to manufacture aluminium.

• The aluminium oxide is mixed with molten cryolite to lower its melting point.

• Aluminium forms at the negative electrode and oxygen at the positive electrode.

• The positive carbon electrodes are replaced regularly as they gradually burn away.

AQA Examiner's tip

You do not need to know the formula of cryolite, just that it is used to lower the operating temperature of the electrolysis cell to make it possible to electrolyse aluminium oxide and to save energy.

• Aluminium is more reactive than carbon and so it must be extracted from its ore by electrolysis. Its ore contains aluminium oxide which must be purified and then melted so that it can be electrolysed. Aluminium oxide melts at over 2000 °C, which would need a lot of energy. Aluminium oxide is mixed with another ionic compound called cryolite, so that the mixture melts at about 850 °C. The mixture can be electrolysed at this lower temperature and produces aluminium and oxygen as the products.

▶ **1** *Why is aluminium oxide mixed with cryolite in the electrolysis cell?*

• The overall reaction in the electrolysis cell is:

$$\text{aluminium oxide} \rightarrow \text{aluminium} + \text{oxygen}$$
$$2Al_2O_3(l) \rightarrow 4Al(l) + 3O_2(g)$$

• The cryolite remains in the cell and fresh aluminium oxide is added as aluminium and oxygen are produced.

• At the negative electrode aluminium ions are reduced to aluminium atoms by gaining electrons. The molten aluminium metal is collected from the bottom of the cell.

• At the positive electrode oxide ions are oxidised to oxygen atoms by losing electrons and the oxygen atoms form oxygen molecules.

▶ **2** *What are the final products of the electrolysis cell?*

Half equations

At the negative electrode: $Al^{3+}(l) + 3e^- \rightarrow Al(l)$

At the positive electrode: $2O^{2-}(l) \rightarrow 2O_2(g) + 4e^-$

• The positive electrodes used in the cell are made of carbon. At the high temperature of the cell the oxygen reacts with the carbon electrodes to produce carbon dioxide. This means that the carbon electrodes gradually burn away and so they have to be replaced regularly.

Higher

Student Book
pages 188–189 **C2**

5.7 Electrolysis of brine

● Brine is a solution of sodium chloride in water. The solution contains sodium ions, $Na^+(aq)$, chloride ions, Cl^- (aq), hydrogen ions, $H^+(aq)$, and hydroxide ions, OH^- (aq). When brine is electrolysed hydrogen is produced at the negative electrode from the hydrogen ions. Chlorine is produced at the positive electrode from the chloride ions. This leaves a solution of sodium ions and hydroxide ions, NaOH(aq).

▶ **1** *Why is hydrogen produced when sodium chloride solution is electrolysed?*

Key points

● When we electrolyse brine we get three products – chlorine gas, hydrogen gas and sodium hydroxide solution.

● The products are important reactants used in industry.

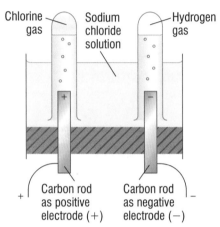

Electrolysis of sodium chloride solution

Half equations

The half equations for the reactions at the electrodes are:

At the positive electrode: $2Cl^- \rightarrow Cl_2 + 2e^-$

At the negative electrode: $2H^+ + 2e^- \rightarrow H_2$

● Sodium hydroxide is a strong alkali and has many uses including making soap, making paper, making bleach, neutralising acids and controlling pH.

● Chlorine is used to kill bacteria in drinking water and in swimming pools, and to make bleach, disinfectants and plastics.

● Hydrogen is used to make margarine and hydrochloric acid.

▶ **2** *Why is the electrolysis of brine an important industrial process?*

Student Book
pages 190–191 **C2**

5.8 Electroplating

Electroplating uses electrolysis to put a thin coating of metal onto an object. Gold, silver and chromium plating are often used. Electroplating can be done for several reasons that may include:

● to make the object look more attractive
● to protect a metal object from corroding
● to increase the hardness of a surface
● to reduce costs by using a thin layer of metal instead of the pure metal.

▶ **1** *Why are some knives, forks and spoons silver-plated?*

● For electroplating, the object to be plated is used as the negative electrode. The positive electrode is made from the plating metal. The electrolyte is a solution containing ions of the plating metal. At the positive electrode, atoms of the plating metal lose electrons to form metal ions which go into the solution. At the negative electrode, metal ions from the solution gain electrons to form metal atoms which are deposited on the object to be plated.

Key points

● We can electroplate objects to improve their appearance, protect their surface, and to use smaller amounts of precious metals.

● The object to be electroplated is made the negative electrode in an electrolysis cell. The plating metal is made the positive electrode. The electrolyte contains ions of the plating metal.

AQA *Examiner's tip*

For electroplating the positive electrode is not inert – it produces ions of the metal used to plate the object.

Half equations for nickel electroplating

At the positive nickel electrode: $Ni(s) \rightarrow Ni^{2+}(aq) + 2e^-$
At the negative electrode to be plated: $Ni^{2+}(aq) + 2e^- \rightarrow Ni(s)$

▶ **2** *Describe how you would silver plate a small piece of copper jewellery.*

1 Dilute nitric acid is added to sodium hydroxide solution.

    a What type of substance is sodium hydroxide?

    b What type of reaction happens?

    c Why is an indicator used to show when the reaction is complete?

    d Write a word equation for the reaction.

2 Describe the main steps to make zinc sulfate crystals from zinc oxide and dilute sulfuric acid.

3 Describe how you could make some insoluble lead sulfate from solutions of lead nitrate and sodium sulfate.

4 Why are some items of jewellery made of gold-plated nickel?

5 Name the products when sodium chloride solution is electrolysed and give one use for each.

6 Aluminium is manufactured from aluminium oxide, Al_2O_3, which is inexpensive.

    a Why is manufacturing aluminium an expensive process?

    b Why is cryolite used in the process to make aluminium?

7 Explain as fully as you can what happens at the electrodes when molten sodium chloride is electrolysed.

8 Write half equations for the reactions at the electrodes when magnesium chloride solution $MgCl_2(aq)$ is electrolysed using carbon electrodes. [H]

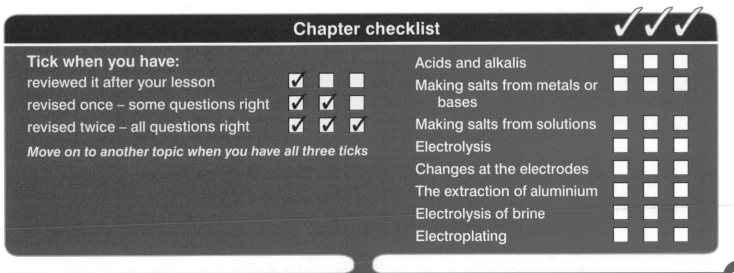

Chapter checklist	✓ ✓ ✓
Tick when you have:	
reviewed it after your lesson ✓ ☐ ☐	Acids and alkalis ☐ ☐ ☐
revised once – some questions right ✓ ✓ ☐	Making salts from metals or bases ☐ ☐ ☐
revised twice – all questions right ✓ ✓ ✓	Making salts from solutions ☐ ☐ ☐
Move on to another topic when you have all three ticks	Electrolysis ☐ ☐ ☐
	Changes at the electrodes ☐ ☐ ☐
	The extraction of aluminium ☐ ☐ ☐
	Electrolysis of brine ☐ ☐ ☐
	Electroplating ☐ ☐ ☐

1 Lithium reacts with fluorine to produce lithium fluoride:

$2Li(s) + F_2(g) \rightarrow 2LiF(s)$

  a For each substance in the equation choose the type of bonding it has from this list: ionic, covalent, metallic. *(3 marks)*

  b Which of the substances in the equation is made of small molecules? *(1 mark)*

  c Which of the substances in the equation would you expect to conduct electricity:
i when solid   **ii** when molten? *(2 marks)*

  d A lithium atom can be represented as shown:

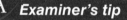

    i   Draw a similar diagram to show a fluorine atom. *(1 mark)*
    ii   Use similar diagrams to show the bonding in lithium fluoride. *(4 marks)*

  e Lithium nanoparticles are used in some batteries.
    i   What is meant by the term nanoparticle? *(1 mark)*
    ii   Suggest **one** advantage of using lithium nanoparticles instead of normal lithium. *(1 mark)*

  f Explain how the atoms are held together in solid lithium. **[H]** *(4 marks)*

2 Calcium hydrogenphosphate, $CaHPO_4$, is used as a dietary supplement in breakfast cereals.

  a Calculate the formula mass, M_r, of $CaHPO_4$.
(Relative atomic masses: Ca = 40, H = 1, P = 31, O = 16) *(2 marks)*

  b Calculate the percentage of calcium in $CaHPO_4$. *(2 marks)*

  c Calcium carbonate, $CaCO_3$, is also used as a dietary supplement. Which compound provides more calcium per 100 g? Show your working.
(Relative atomic mass of C = 12) *(2 marks)*

  d Calcium hydrogenphosphate contains atoms of the isotope $^{31}_{15}P$. Another isotope of phosphorus is $^{32}_{15}P$.
Explain what is meant by the term isotope using these two types of phosphorus atoms as examples. *(3 marks)*

  e An oxide of phosphorus contains 43.7% phosphorus. Calculate the empirical formula of this oxide. **[H]** *(4 marks)*

3 Ammonia is made in industry from nitrogen and hydrogen. The reaction can be represented by the equation:

$$N_2(g) + 3H_2(g) \rightleftharpoons 2NH_3(g)$$

  a What does the symbol $\rightleftharpoons$ tell you about this reaction? *(1 mark)*

  b Draw a dot and cross diagram to show the bonding in a molecule of ammonia. *(2 marks)*

  c Ammonia dissolves in water and reacts to produce an alkaline solution.
$$NH_3(g) + H_2O(l) \rightarrow NH_4^+(aq) + OH^-(aq)$$
How can you tell from the equation that the solution is alkaline? *(1 mark)*

d The soluble salt ammonium nitrate can be made by reacting ammonia solution with dilute nitric acid. The reaction can be represented by the equation:

$$NH_4^+(aq) + OH^-(aq) + H^+(aq) + NO_3^-(aq) \rightarrow NH_4^+(aq) + NO_3^-(aq) + H_2O(l)$$

    i   Write this equation in its simplest form. *(1 mark)*

    ii   What type of reaction is this? *(1 mark)*

    iii *In this question you will be assessed on using good English, organising information clearly and using specialist terms where appropriate.*

        Describe how you would make some ammonium nitrate crystals in the laboratory. You should include a risk assessment in your answer. *(6 marks)*

e The reaction can also be represented by this equation: **[H]**

$$NH_3(aq) + HNO_3(aq) \rightarrow NH_4NO_3(aq)$$

    i   Calculate the maximum mass of ammonium nitrate that can be made from 1.7 g of ammonia. (Relative atomic masses: H = 1, N = 14, O = 16) *(3 marks)*

    ii   A student made 5.2 g of ammonium nitrate crystals from 1.7 g of ammonia. What was the percentage yield? *(2 marks)*

4 Some types of hand warmers use the reaction of iron with oxygen:

$$4Fe(s) + 3O_2(g) \rightarrow 2Fe_2O_3(s)$$

The hand warmers contain iron powder moistened with salt solution. The salt acts as a catalyst. When air is allowed into the mixture it reacts with the iron and the pack gets warm. The hand warmers can work for several hours.

a What type of reaction transfers energy to the surroundings? *(1 mark)*

b What is meant by a catalyst? *(2 marks)*

c Suggest **two** ways, other than increasing the temperature, that could be used to make the reaction in the hand warmer go faster. *(2 marks)*

5 A student electrolysed some sodium chloride solution using the apparatus shown in the diagram.

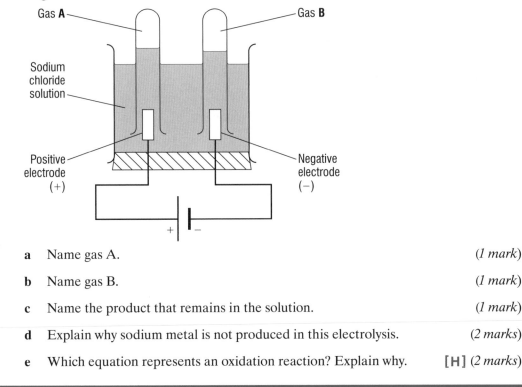

a Name gas A. *(1 mark)*

b Name gas B. *(1 mark)*

c Name the product that remains in the solution. *(1 mark)*

d Explain why sodium metal is not produced in this electrolysis. *(2 marks)*

e Which equation represents an oxidation reaction? Explain why. **[H]** *(2 marks)*

AQA **Examiner's tip**

In questions like 3 d iii that give marks for quality of written communication, plan your answer by writing brief notes of the main steps, make sure these are in a sensible order and then write your answer.

1.1 The early periodic table

- During the 19th century, many elements had been discovered but scientists did not know about the structure of atoms. Scientists tried to find ways to classify the elements based on their properties and **atomic weights**.

> **1** *Why did scientists in the 19th century use atomic weights rather than proton numbers to classify the elements?*

- In 1863 Newlands proposed his law of octaves, which stated that similar properties are repeated every eighth element. He put the 62 elements known at that time into seven groups according to their atomic weights. After calcium their properties did not match very well within the groups and so other scientists did not accept his ideas.

- In 1869 Mendeleev produced a better table. He left gaps for undiscovered elements so that the groups of known elements did have similar properties. He predicted the properties of the missing elements. When some of the missing elements were discovered, Mendeleev's predictions were confirmed and then other scientists more readily accepted his ideas. Mendeleev's table became the basis for the modern **periodic table**.

> **2** *Why was Mendeleev's table better than Newlands' table?*

AQA Examiner's tip

You may have studied the work of other scientists in developing the periodic table but you only need to know about the work of Newlands and Mendeleev for the exam. You do not need to remember details of the early tables.

Key points

- The periodic table of the elements developed as chemists tried to classify the elements. It arranges them in a pattern in which similar elements are grouped together.

- Newlands' table put the elements in order of atomic weight but failed to take account of elements that were unknown at that time.

- Mendeleev's periodic table left gaps for the unknown elements, and so provided the basis for the modern periodic table.

Dmitri Mendeleev together with a Russian stamp issued in his honour in 1969

Typische Elemente			K = 39	Rb = 85	Cs = 133	—	—
			Ca = 40	Sr = 87	Ba = 137	—	—
			—	?Yt = 88?	?Di = 138?	Er = 178?	—
			Ti = 48?	Zr = 90	Ce = 140?	?La = 180?	Tb = 231
			V = 51	Nb = 94	—	Ta = 182	—
			Cr = 52	Mo = 96	—	W = 184	U = 240
			Mn = 55	—	—	—	—
			Fe = 56	Ru = 104	—	Os = 195?	—
			Co = 59	Rh = 104	—	Ir = 197	—
			Ni = 59	Pd = 106	—	Pt = 198?	—
H = 1	Li = 7	Na = 23	Cu = 63	Ag = 108	—	Au = 199?	—
	Be = 9,4	Mg = 24	Zn = 65	Cd = 112	—	Hg = 200	—
	B = 11	Al = 27,3	—	In = 113	—	Tl = 204	—
	C = 12	Si = 28	—	Sn = 118	—	Pb = 207	—
	N = 14	P = 31	As = 75	Sb = 122	—	Bi = 208	—
	O = 16	S = 32	Se = 78	Te = 125?	—	—	—
	F = 19	Cl = 35,5	Br = 80	J = 127	—	—	—

An early version of Mendeleev's periodic table with similar elements arranged horizontally in rows

Key words: atomic weight, periodic table

1.2 The modern periodic table

Key points

- The atomic (proton) number of an element determines its position in the periodic table.

- The number of electrons in the outermost shell (highest energy level) of an atom determines its chemical properties.

- The group number in the periodic table equals the number of electrons in the outermost shell.

- We can explain trends in reactivity as we go down a group in terms of:
  - the distance between the outermost electrons and the nucleus
  - the number of occupied inner shells (energy levels) in the atoms.   [H]

- Scientists found out about protons and electrons at the start of the 20th century. Soon after this, they developed models of the arrangement of electrons in atoms. The elements were arranged in the periodic table in order of their atomic numbers (proton numbers) and were lined up in vertical **groups**.

- The groups of elements have similar chemical properties because their atoms have the same number of electrons in their highest occupied energy level (outer shell). For the main groups, the number of electrons in the outer shell is the same as the group number.

▐▶ **1** *Why do elements in a group have similar chemical properties?*

Reactivity within groups

Within a group the reactivity of the elements depends on the total number of electrons. Going down a group, there are more occupied energy levels and the atoms get larger. As the atoms get larger, the electrons in the highest occupied energy level (outer shell) are less strongly attracted by the nucleus.

- When metals react they lose electrons, so the reactivity of metals in a group increases going down the group.

- When non-metals react they gain electrons, so the reactivity of non-metals decreases going down a group.

▐▶ **2** *Why do metals get more reactive going down a group?*

Bump up your grade

You should be able to explain the trends in reactivity in the main groups in the periodic table in terms of electronic structure.

AQA Examiner's tip

You may describe electron arrangements in terms of energy levels or shells. The term 'outer electrons' is generally accepted as referring to the electrons in the highest occupied energy level or outer shell.

Group numbers

Relative atomic mass
Atomic (proton) number

1	2											3	4	5	6	7	0
						1 **H** 1											4 **He** 2
7 **Li** 3	9 **Be** 4											11 **B** 5	12 **C** 6	14 **N** 7	16 **O** 8	19 **F** 9	20 **Ne** 10
23 **Na** 11	24 **Mg** 12											27 **Al** 13	28 **Si** 14	31 **P** 15	32 **S** 16	35.5 **Cl** 17	40 **Ar** 18
39 **K** 19	40 **Ca** 20	45 **Sc** 21	48 **Ti** 22	51 **V** 23	52 **Cr** 24	55 **Mn** 25	56 **Fe** 26	59 **Co** 27	59 **Ni** 28	63.5 **Cu** 29	65 **Zn** 30	70 **Ga** 31	73 **Ge** 32	75 **As** 33	79 **Se** 34	80 **Br** 35	84 **Kr** 36
85 **Rb** 37	88 **Sr** 38	89 **Y** 39	91 **Zr** 40	93 **Nb** 41	96 **Mo** 42	98 **Tc** 43	101 **Ru** 44	103 **Rh** 45	106 **Pd** 46	108 **Ag** 47	112 **Cd** 48	115 **In** 49	119 **Sn** 50	122 **Sb** 51	128 **Te** 52	127 **I** 53	131 **Xe** 54
133 **Cs** 55	137 **Ba** 56	139 **La** 57	178 **Hf** 72	181 **Ta** 73	184 **W** 74	186 **Re** 75	190 **Os** 76	192 **Ir** 77	195 **Pt** 78	197 **Au** 79	201 **Hg** 80	204 **Tl** 81	207 **Pb** 82	209 **Bi** 83	209 **Po** 84	210 **At** 85	222 **Rn** 86
223 **Fr** 87	226 **Ra** 88	227 **Ac** 89															

Elements 58–71 and 90–103 (all metals) have been omitted

The modern periodic table

Student Book
pages 200–201 **C3**

1.3 Group 1 – the alkali metals

- The Group 1 elements are called the **alkali metals**. They are all metals that react readily with air and water.
- They are soft solids at room temperature with low melting and boiling points that decrease going down the group. They have low densities, so lithium, sodium and potassium float on water.
- They react with water to produce hydrogen gas and a metal hydroxide that is an alkali, e.g.

$$\text{sodium} + \text{water} \rightarrow \text{sodium hydroxide} + \text{hydrogen}$$
$$2Na(s) + 2H_2O(l) \rightarrow 2NaOH(aq) + H_2(g)$$

▶ **1** *Why are the elements in Group 1 called 'alkali metals'?*

- They all have one electron in their highest occupied energy level (outer shell). They lose this electron in reactions to form ionic compounds in which their ions have a single positive charge, e.g. Na^+.
- They react with the halogens (Group 7) to form salts that are white or colourless crystals, e.g.

$$\text{sodium} + \text{chlorine} \rightarrow \text{sodium chloride}$$
$$2Na(s) + Cl_2(g) \rightarrow 2NaCl(s)$$

- Compounds of alkali metals dissolve in water, forming solutions that are usually colourless.
- Going down Group 1, the reactivity of the alkali metals increases.

▶ **2** *Name and give the formula of the compound formed when potassium reacts with bromine.*

Key points

- The elements in Group 1 of the periodic table are called the alkali metals.
- These metals all react with water to produce hydrogen and an alkaline solution containing the metal hydroxide.
- They form positive ions with a charge of 1+ in reactions to make ionic compounds. Their compounds are usually white or colourless crystals that dissolve in water producing colourless solutions.
- The reactivity of the alkali metals increases going down the group.

AQA Examiner's tip

The alkali metals form only ionic compounds in which their ions have a single positive charge.

Explanation of reactivity trend in Group 1

Reactivity increases going down Group 1 because the outer electron is less strongly attracted to the nucleus as the number of occupied energy levels increases and the atoms get larger.

▶ **3** *Why is lithium less reactive than sodium?*

Bump up your grade

If you are taking the Higher Tier paper, you should be able to explain the trend in reactivity in Group 1 in terms of electronic structure.

Key word: alkali metal

7
Li
3
23
Na
11
39
K
19
85
Rb
37
113
Cs
55
223
Fr
87

The alkali metals (Group 1)

Student Book
pages 202–203

C3

1.4 The transition elements

- The **transition elements** are found in the periodic table between Groups 2 and 3.
- They are all metals and so are sometimes called the **transition metals**.

45 Sc 21	48 **Ti** 22	51 V 23	52 **Cr** 24	55 **Mn** 25	56 **Fe** 26	59 **Co** 27	59 **Ni** 28	63 **Cu** 29	64 **Zn** 30
89 Y 39	91 Zr 40	93 Nb 41	96 Mo 42	99 Tc 43	101 Ru 44	103 Rh 45	106 Pd 46	108 **Ag** 47	112 Cd 48
	178 Hf 72	181 Ta 73	184 W 74	186 Re 75	190 Os 76	192 Ir 77	195 **Pt** 78	197 **Au** 79	201 **Hg** 80

The transition elements. The more common elements are shown in bold type.

- Except for mercury, they have higher melting and boiling points than the alkali metals.
- They are malleable and ductile and they are good conductors of heat and electricity.
- They react only slowly, or not at all, with oxygen and water at ordinary temperatures.
- Most are strong and dense and are useful as building materials, often as alloys.

▶ **1** *Why are transition metals useful as building materials?*

- They form positive ions with various charges, e.g. Fe^{2+} and Fe^{3+}.
- Compounds of transition metals are often brightly coloured.
- Many transition metals and their compounds are catalysts for chemical reactions.

▶ **2** *List the ways in which transition elements are different from the elements in Group 1.*

Key points

- Compared with the alkali metals, transition elements have much higher melting points and densities. They are also stronger and harder, but are much less reactive.
- The transition elements do not react vigorously with oxygen or water.
- Transition elements can form ions with different charges, in compounds that are often coloured.
- Transition elements and their compounds are important industrial catalysts.

Bump up your grade

For your exam, try to remember how to write formulae for transition metal compounds. If you are taking the Higher Tier paper you should also be able to balance equations for the reactions of transition metals.

AQA Examiner's tip

The charge on a transition metal ion is given by the Roman numeral in its name. For example, iron(II) chloride contains Fe^{2+} ions and so its formula is $FeCl_2$ and iron(III) chloride contains Fe^{3+} ions and its formula is $FeCl_3$.

Transition metals are used as building materials, e.g. iron is used in the steel in this bridge

Key words: transition element, transition metals

Student Book
pages 204–205

C3

1.5 Group 7 – the halogens

- The **halogens** are non-metallic elements in Group 7 of the periodic table.
- They exist as small molecules made up of pairs of atoms. They have low melting and boiling points that increase going down the group. At room temperature fluorine is a pale yellow gas, chlorine is a green gas, bromine is a red-brown liquid and iodine is a grey solid. Iodine easily vaporises to a violet gas.

> **1** *Why do the halogens have low melting and boiling points?*

- All of the halogens have seven electrons in their highest occupied energy level.
- The halogens form ionic compounds with metals in which the **halide ions** have a charge of 1–.
- The halogens also bond covalently with non-metals, forming molecules.
- The reactivity of the halogens decreases going down the group. A more reactive halogen is able to displace a less reactive halogen from an aqueous solution of a halide compound.

> **2** *How could you show that chlorine is more reactive than bromine?*

Explanation of reactivity trend for Group 7

The reactivity of the halogens decreases going down Group 7 because the attraction of the outer electrons to the nucleus decreases as the number of occupied energy levels (shells) increases.

AQA Examiner's tip

Make sure you revise ionic and covalent bonding so you are clear about the differences in properties between ionic compounds and covalent compounds that have small molecules.

Bump up your grade

If you are taking the Higher Tier paper, you should be able to explain the trend in reactivity in Group 7 in terms of electronic structure.

Key points

- The halogens all form ions with a single negative charge in their ionic compounds with metals.
- The halogens form covalent compounds by sharing electrons with other non-metals.
- A more reactive halogen can displace a less reactive halogen from a solution of one of its salts.
- The reactivity of the halogens decreases going down the group.

19	
	F
9	
35	
	Cl
17	
80	
	Br
35	
127	
	I
53	
210	
	At
85	

The Group 7 elements, the halogens

Chlorine, bromine and iodine

1 What was Newlands' law of octaves?

2 How was Mendeleev's periodic table an improvement on Newlands' table?

3 Why do elements in the groups in the modern periodic table have similar properties?

4 A small piece of lithium is added to a bowl of water.

    a   Write a word equation for the reaction of lithium with water.

    b   Describe three things that you would see when the lithium is added to the water.

    c   How could you show that an alkali is produced?

    d   Give one way in which the reaction of sodium with water is different to the reaction of lithium with water.

5 Predict three physical and three chemical properties of the transition element cobalt, Co.

6 What is the trend in melting points and boiling points going down Group 7?

7 What is the formula of sodium bromide? Describe its appearance and what happens when it is mixed with water.

8 Hydrogen chloride is a gas at room temperature. Explain why.

9 Some chlorine water was added to an aqueous solution of potassium bromide.

    a   Describe the colour change that you would see.

    b   Write a word equation for the reaction that happens.

    c   Write a balanced symbol equation for the reaction.   [H]

10 Iron reacts with chlorine to produce iron(III) chloride. Write a balanced symbol equation for this reaction.   [H]

11 Explain in terms of electronic structures:

    a   why sodium is more reactive than lithium

    b   why fluorine is more reactive than chlorine.   [H]

Chapter checklist	✓ ✓ ✓

Tick when you have:							
reviewed it after your lesson	✓	☐	☐	The early periodic table	☐	☐	☐
revised once – some questions right	✓	✓	☐	The modern periodic table	☐	☐	☐
revised twice – all questions right	✓	✓	✓	Group 1 – the alkali metals	☐	☐	☐
Move on to another topic when you have all three ticks				The transition elements	☐	☐	☐
				Group 7 – the halogens	☐	☐	☐

Student Book
pages 208–209 **C3**

2.1 Hard water

Key points

- Hard water contains dissolved compounds such as calcium and magnesium salts.

- The calcium and/or magnesium ions in hard water react with soap producing a precipitate called scum.

- Temporary hard water can produce a solid scale when it is heated, reducing the efficiency of heating systems and kettles.

- Hard water is better than soft water for developing and maintaining teeth and bones. It may also help to prevent heart disease.

Scum is left in the sink after using soap with hard water

- Water that lathers easily with soap is said to be **soft water**. **Hard water** uses more soap to produce lather and to wash effectively. This is because hard water contains dissolved compounds that react with soap to form an insoluble solid called **scum**. Other detergents, called **soapless detergents**, do not react with hard water to form scum.

➡ **1** *What is the difference between soft water and hard water?*

- When water is in contact with rocks some compounds dissolve. If the water contains dissolved calcium or magnesium ions, these will react with soap to form scum and so the water is hard.

- When it is heated, one type of hard water called temporary hard water produces an insoluble solid called **scale**. Scale can be deposited in kettles, boilers and pipes. This reduces the efficiency of heating systems and causing blockages.

➡ **2** *What is the difference between scum and scale?*

- Calcium compounds are good for our health, helping to develop strong bones and teeth. Calcium may also reduce the risk of heart disease.

➡ **3** *Why is it better to drink hard water rather than soft water?*

AQA *Examiner's tip*

Many candidates confuse scum and scale. **S**cu**m** is formed when **s**oap reacts with dissolved co**m**pounds in hard water. When temporary hard water is heated it produces **scale** which **covers** pipes and heating elements (**scales cover fish**).

As scale builds up in heating systems and kettles it not only makes them less efficient – it can stop them working completely

---

Key words: soft water, hard water, scum, soapless detergent, scale

Key points

- Soft water does not contain salts that produce scum or scale.

- Hard water can be softened by removing the salts that produce scum and scale.

- Temporary hardness is removed from water by heating it. Permanent hardness is not changed by heating.

- The hydrogencarbonate ions in temporary hard water decompose on heating. The carbonate ions formed react with Ca^{2+}(aq) and Mg^{2+}(aq), making precipitates. **[H]**

- Both types of hard water can be softened by adding washing soda or by using an ion-exchange resin to remove calcium and magnesium ions.

AQA *Examiner's tip*

Any method that removes dissolved calcium and magnesium ions from hard water will soften the water.

Washing soda is a simple way to soften water

2.2 Removing hardness

- Soft water may contain dissolved substances but it does not contain dissolved salts that react with soap to produce scum. Also, it does not produce scale when it is heated.

- Hard water can be made soft by removing the dissolved calcium and magnesium ions that react with soap.

- Some types of hard water are affected by heating while others are not. **Temporary hard water** is softened by boiling because when it is heated the calcium and magnesium compounds form insoluble scale and this removes them from the water. **Permanent hard water** is not softened by boiling and does not produce scale when it is heated.

▶ **1** *What is meant by 'temporary hard water'?*

How temporary hard water is softened by heating

Temporary hard water contains hydrogencarbonate ions, HCO_3^-(aq). The hydrogencarbonate ions decompose when heated to produce carbonate ions, water and carbon dioxide: $2HCO_3^-$(aq) $\rightarrow CO_3^{2-}$(aq) $+ H_2O$(l) $+CO_2$(g)

The carbonate ions react with calcium ions and magnesium ions in the water to produce precipitates of calcium carbonate and magnesium carbonate that are deposited as scale.

▶ **2** *Write a balanced equation, including state symbols, for the reaction of calcium ions with carbonate ions.*

- One method of softening either type of hard water is by precipitating out the ions that cause hardness. This can be done by adding washing soda, which is sodium carbonate. The sodium carbonate reacts with calcium ions and magnesium ions in the water to form solid calcium carbonate and magnesium carbonate that cannot react with soap.

- Another method is to use an **ion-exchange column** packed with a resin containing sodium or hydrogen ions. When hard water is passed through the resin, calcium and magnesium ions become attached to the resin and sodium ions or hydrogen ions take their place in the water. Sodium ions and hydrogen ions do not react with soap.

▶ **3** *How does an ion-exchange resin soften hard water?*

> ### Bump up your grade
>
> If you are taking the Higher Tier paper, you should be able to explain and write equations for the reactions that happen when temporary hard water is heated.

Key words: temporary hard water, permanent hard water, ion-exchange column

Higher

Student Book
pages 212–213 **C3**

2.3 Water treatment

- Drinking water should not contain any harmful substances and should have sufficiently low levels of dissolved salts and microbes.

- Water from an appropriate source can be treated to make it safe to drink. Water is often treated by sedimentation and filtration to remove solids. This is followed by disinfection to kill microbes in the water. Chlorine is often used to kill microbes in drinking water.

▐▐▐➤ **1** *How is drinking water treated to make it safe to drink?*

- Water filters can be used to improve the taste of water. They often contain carbon and an ion-exchange resin that remove some soluble substances and silver or another substance to prevent the growth of bacteria.

- Pure water can be made by distillation. This requires a large amount of energy to boil the water and so it would be very expensive to do on a large scale.

▐▐▐➤ **2** *Explain why distillation is not used to treat mains tap water.*

AQA Examiner's tip

Many people think that drinking water must be pure water. It does not have to be pure, but it should not contain anything that will cause us harm.

Bump up your grade

You should know the three main stages involved in producing water that is fit to drink: suitable source, removal of solids, killing of microbes.

Key points

- Water for drinking should contain only low levels of dissolved substances and microbes.
- Water is made fit to drink by filtering it to remove solids and adding chlorine to kill microbes.
- We can make pure water by distillation but this requires large amounts of energy which makes it expensive.

Good, clean water is a precious resource. Those of us lucky enough to have it can too easily take it for granted.

Student Book
pages 214–215 **C3**

2.4 Water issues

- When water is treated, there are advantages and disadvantages. These must be carefully considered before any decision to treat water is taken. This is particularly important for the treatment of public water supplies.

- The hardness of the water supplied depends on where you live. Hard water causes problems in heating systems and with washing, but if used for drinking has health benefits. If the water is not suitable for a particular purpose you can treat the water or use an alternative supply.

▐▐▐➤ **1** *Suggest one advantage and one disadvantage of softening hard water.*

- Chlorine is particularly effective in killing microbes in water so that it is safe to use. However, chlorine is poisonous, and it can produce other toxic compounds. Therefore its use must be carefully controlled to minimise the risks.

- Fluoride compounds are added to toothpastes and to water supplies to help prevent tooth decay. The arguments for and against adding fluorides to water supplies are complicated. One of the arguments against adding fluoride to water is that people should be able to choose to take extra fluoride or not.

▐▐▐➤ **2** *What would be the consequences of not adding chlorine and fluoride to tap water?*

Key points

- There are advantages and disadvantages to any type of water treatment.
- Water can be treated to remove hardness, to remove harmful microbes and to improve dental health.

AQA Examiner's tip

You should understand the principles of water treatment described in the specification but you do not need to remember any specific details of other methods. However, you should be prepared to evaluate any information you are given about water treatment methods.

1. Why does hard water produce scum?

2. What is produced when temporary hard water is heated?

3. Give one advantage of drinking hard water.

4. Explain the difference between temporary hard water and permanent hard water.

5. How does washing soda soften hard water?

6. Give one disadvantage of using a sodium ion-exchange resin to soften hard water.

7. What type of substance is removed from water at a treatment works by filtration?

8. Why is chlorine used in water treatment?

9. Why is it not necessary to distil water used for drinking?

10. Why are fluorides added to drinking water?

11. Explain what happens when temporary hard water is boiled. Include two balanced symbol equations in your answer. [H]

Chapter checklist			✔ ✔ ✔
Tick when you have:			Hard water ☐ ☐ ☐
reviewed it after your lesson	✔ ☐ ☐		Removing hardness ☐ ☐ ☐
revised once – some questions right	✔ ✔ ☐		Water treatment ☐ ☐ ☐
revised twice – all questions right	✔ ✔ ✔		Water issues ☐ ☐ ☐
Move on to another topic when you have all three ticks			

3.1 Comparing the energy released by fuels

Key points

- When fuels and food react with oxygen, energy is released in an exothermic reaction.

- A simple calorimeter can be used to compare the energy released by different fuels or different foods in a school lab.

Bump up your grade

Remember that you can calculate the energy released by burning a fuel using the equation $Q = mc\Delta T$. If you are taking the Higher Tier paper, you should be able to calculate the energy released by burning a known mass of fuel in kJ/g and, when given the formula of the fuel or its relative formula mass, in kJ/mol.

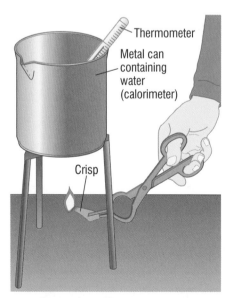

The energy released by fuels and foods when they burn can be compared using some very simple equipment

- When fuels and foods react with oxygen the reactions are exothermic. Different amounts of energy are released by different fuels and foods. The amount of energy released is usually measured in joules (J), but sometimes values are given in calories (1 cal = 4.2 J).

- We can use a calorimeter to measure the amount of energy released when substances burn. The simplest calorimeter is some water in a glass beaker or metal can. When a substance burns and heats the water, the temperature rise of the water depends on the amount of energy released.

- The amount of energy transferred to the water can be calculated using the equation:

$$Q = mc\Delta T$$

Where:
Q is the amount of energy transferred to the water in joules, J
m is the mass of water in grams, g
c is the specific heat capacity of water in J/g °C
ΔT is the temperature change in °C.

Maths skills

Worked example

0.50 g of a fuel was burned and used to heat 200 g of water in a calorimeter. The temperature of the water increased by 14 °C. The specific heat capacity of water, c = 4.2 J/g °C

Using $Q = mc\Delta T$ Energy released = 200 × 4.2 × 14 = 11 760 J = 11.76 kJ
Energy released per g of fuel = 11.76/0.5 = 23.52 kJ/g

> **1**   *0.45 g of fuel A was burned and heated 150 g of water in a calorimeter. The temperature of the water changed from 19 °C to 45 °C. How much energy was released by 1.0 g of fuel?*

- Simple calorimeters do not give accurate results for the energy released because much of it is used to heat the surroundings. However, the results can be used to compare the energy released by different fuels.

- To compare the energy released by burning different substances either the energy change in kJ per gram or the energy change in kJ per mole can be used.

- The energy change in kJ/mol can be calculated by multiplying the energy change in kJ/g by the relative formula mass of the substance.

> **2**   *In a similar experiment to that in Question 1, fuel B released 35.6 kJ/g. The relative formula mass of fuel A is 72 and fuel B is 114. Which fuel releases more energy per mole?*

AQA Examiner's tip

You do not need to remember the specific heat capacity of water or the value used to convert joules into calories because these will be given in any question when you need to use them.

Student Book
pages 220–221

C3

3.2 Energy transfers in solutions

Key points

- We can calculate the energy change for reactions in solution by measuring the temperature change and using the equation:

  $Q = mc\Delta T$

- Neutralisation and displacement reactions are both examples of reactions that we can use this technique for.

AQA **Examiner's tip**

For reactions in aqueous solutions, remember to use only the volume of the solution when calculating the energy change and assume that the specific heat capacity of any aqueous solution is the same as water.

- When a reaction takes place in solution, energy is transferred to or from the solution.
- We can do the reactions in an insulated container to reduce energy transfers to the surroundings.
- We can measure the temperature change of the solution and use this to calculate the energy change using the equation $Q = mc\Delta T$.
- In these calculations we assume the solutions behave like water. This means that 1 cm³ of solution has a mass of 1 g and the specific heat capacity of the solution is 4.2 J/g °C.

Maths skills

Worked example

A student added 25 cm³ of dilute nitric acid to 25 cm³ of potassium hydroxide solution in a polystyrene cup. He recorded a temperature rise of 12 °C. Calculate the energy change.

$Q = mc\Delta T$ Volume of solution = 25 + 25 = 50 cm³

Energy change = 50 × 4.2 × 12

    = 2520 J = 2.52 kJ

▶ 1   *When 50 cm³ of sulfuric acid was added to 100 cm³ of sodium hydroxide in a polystyrene cup the temperature increased by 12 °C. Calculate the energy change.*

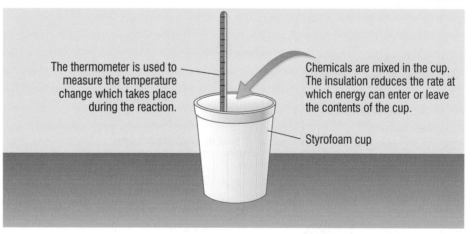

The thermometer is used to measure the temperature change which takes place during the reaction.

Chemicals are mixed in the cup. The insulation reduces the rate at which energy can enter or leave the contents of the cup.

Styrofoam cup

A simple calorimeter can be used to measure energy changes in solution

- When a solid is added to water or to an aqueous solution we assume that the volume of the solution does not change. We also assume that 1 cm³ of solution has a mass of 1 g and that its specific heat capacity is 4.2 J/g °C.
- If we know the number of moles involved in the reaction for which we have calculated the energy change we can calculate the energy change for the reaction in kJ/mol.

▶ 2   *When 5.6 g of iron filings reacted completely with 200 cm³ of copper(II) sulfate solution the temperature of the solution increased by 17 °C. Calculate the energy change in kJ/mol of iron. (Relative atomic mass of Fe = 56)*

3.3 Energy level diagrams

- We can show the energy changes for chemical reactions on energy level diagrams.
- The difference between the energy levels of reactants and products is the energy change for the reaction.
- The energy level diagram for an exothermic reaction is shown on the left.

▐▌▶ **1** *Draw a similar energy level diagram for an endothermic reaction.*

- During a chemical reaction bonds in the reactants must be broken for the reaction to happen. Breaking bonds is endothermic because energy is taken in.
- The minimum energy needed for the reaction to happen is called the **activation energy**.
- When new bonds in the products are formed, energy is released and so this is exothermic.
- We can show the activation energy and how the energy changes during a reaction on an energy level diagram. This type of diagram is shown below.

▐▌▶ **2** *Draw a similar energy level diagram for an endothermic reaction.*

- Catalysts increase the rate of a reaction by providing a different pathway with an activation energy that is lower. The effect of a catalyst on an exothermic reaction is shown below.

Key points

- We can show the relative difference in the energy of reactants and products on energy level diagrams.
- Catalysts provide a pathway with a lower activation energy so the rate of reaction increases.
- Bond breaking is endothermic and bond making is exothermic.

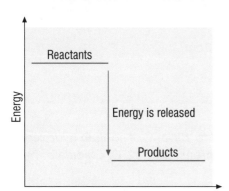

An energy level diagram for an exothermic reaction

Bump up your grade

Learn how to sketch and label energy level diagrams for exothermic and endothermic reactions and show the effect of a catalyst on the activation energy.

AQA Examiner's tip

Remember that energy increases up the diagrams, so endothermic changes (energy in) go up and exothermic changes (energy exits) go down.

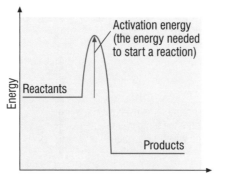

Energy level diagram showing the activation energy for an exothermic reaction

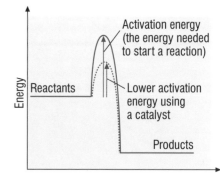

A catalyst provides a different reaction pathway with a lower activation energy

▐▌▶ **3** *Draw an energy level diagram to show the effect of a catalyst on an endothermic reaction.*

Key word: activation energy

3.4 Calculations using bond energies

Key points

● In an exothermic reaction, the energy released when new bonds are formed is greater than the energy absorbed when bonds are broken. **[H]**

● In an endothermic reaction, the energy released when new bonds are formed is less than the energy absorbed when bonds are broken. **[H]**

● We can calculate the overall energy change in a chemical reaction using bond energies. **[H]**

Table of bond energies

Bond	Bond energy in kJ/mol
C–C	347
C–H	413
H–O	464
O=O	498
C=O	805

Bump up your grade

Get plenty of practice at calculating the energy change for a reaction given its balanced equation and values for the bond energies.

Bond energies

In a chemical reaction, energy is needed to break the bonds in the reactants. Energy is released when new bonds are formed in the products. It is the difference in these energy changes that makes the overall reaction exothermic or endothermic.

The energy needed to break the bond between two atoms is called the **bond energy** for that bond. An equal amount of energy is released when the bond forms between two atoms and so we can use bond energies to calculate the overall energy change for a reaction. Bond energies are measured in kJ/mol.

The balanced equation for the reaction is needed to calculate the energy change for a reaction. Then calculate:

● the total amount of energy needed to break all of the bonds in the reactants
● the total amount of energy released in making all of the bonds in the products
● the difference between the two totals.

Maths skills

Worked example
Use the bond energies in the table to calculate the energy change for burning methane:

$$CH_4 + 2O_2 \rightarrow CO_2 + 2H_2O$$

Bonds broken: $4 \times$ C–H $+ 2 \times$ O=O   Energy needed $= (4 \times 413) + (2 \times 498)$
$= 2648\,kJ$

Bonds formed: $2 \times$ C=O $+ 4 \times$ H–O   Energy released $= (2 \times 805) + (4 \times 464)$
$= 3466\,kJ$

Difference $= 3466 - 2648 = 818\,kJ$
Energy change for the reaction $= 818\,kJ/mol$ released

➠ 1 *Calculate the energy change for burning propane:*
$C_3H_8 + 5O_2 \rightarrow 3CO_2 + 4H_2O$

AQA *Examiner's tip*

Bond energies can be found in tables of data. In the examinations you will be given the values for any bond energies that you need to use in the questions. You do not need to know about ΔH or sign conventions for the overall change – but you should be able to decide if the energy change calculated is energy released or energy absorbed (taken in).

Key word: bond energy

3.5 Fuel issues

- Fossil fuels are non-renewable and they cause pollution. The need to develop alternative fuels is becoming more urgent.

- Hydrogen has advantages as a fuel. It burns easily and releases a large amount of energy per gram. It produces no carbon dioxide when it is burned, only water.

- Hydrogen can be burned in combustion engines or can be used in fuel cells to power vehicles.

- Hydrogen can be produced from renewable sources. The disadvantages of using hydrogen include supply, storage and safety problems.

- Vehicles that use fuel cells need to match the performance, convenience and costs of petrol and diesel vehicles.

⟩⟩⟩ **1** *Why are cars fuelled with hydrogen being developed?*

Some hydrogen re-fuelling stations have been set up to trial the use of hydrogen-powered combustion engines in vehicles

A London bus that runs on fuel cells

1 Why do simple calorimeters give inaccurate results for the energy released by burning a fuel?

2 How can you tell from an energy level diagram that a reaction is endothermic?

3 Draw an energy level diagram for the exothermic reaction $CH_4 + 2O_2 \rightarrow CO_2 + 2H_2O$. Show and label the reaction pathway, the activation energy and the energy change of the reaction.

4 0.50 g of a fuel was burned and heated 200 g of water in a calorimeter. The temperature increased by 15 °C. Calculate the energy released by the fuel using the equation $Q = mc\Delta T$, in which $c = 4.2$ J/g °C

5 0.10 mol of zinc was added to 100 cm³ of copper(II) sulfate solution. The temperature increased by 18 °C. Use the equation $Q = mc\Delta T$ to calculate the energy change for the reaction in kJ/mol.

6 100 cm³ of hydrochloric acid containing 0.10 mol of HCl was added to 100 cm³ of sodium hydroxide solution containing 0.10 mol of NaOH. The temperature of the solution increased by 7 °C. Calculate the energy change for this reaction in kJ/mol.

7 Draw and label an energy level diagram with reaction pathways to show the effect of a catalyst on an exothermic reaction.

8 Suggest three problems that need to be overcome to make hydrogen a suitable fuel for cars.

9 Calculate the energy change for the reaction $H_2 + F_2 \rightarrow 2HF$ using bond energies: H–H = 436 kJ/mol, F–F = 158 kJ/mol, H–F = 568 kJ/mol.　　　　[H]

10 Calculate the energy change for the reaction $CH_2=CH_2 + 3O_2 \rightarrow 2CO_2 + 2H_2O$ using bond energies: C–H = 413 kJ/mol , C=C = 612 kJ/mol, O=O = 498 kJ/mol, C=O = 805 kJ/mol, H–O = 464 kJ/mol.　　　　[H]

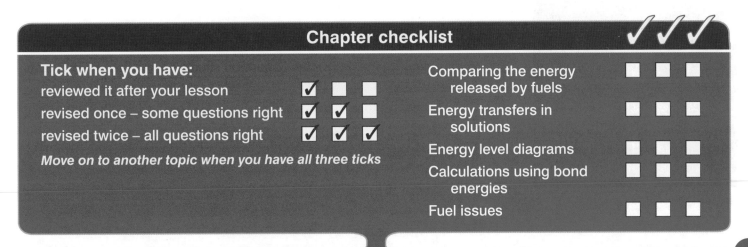

Chapter checklist

Tick when you have:

reviewed it after your lesson　☑ ◻ ◻

revised once – some questions right　☑ ☑ ◻

revised twice – all questions right　☑ ☑ ☑

Move on to another topic when you have all three ticks

Comparing the energy released by fuels　◻ ◻ ◻

Energy transfers in solutions　◻ ◻ ◻

Energy level diagrams　◻ ◻ ◻

Calculations using bond energies　◻ ◻ ◻

Fuel issues　◻ ◻ ◻

Student Book
pages 230–231

C3

4.1 Tests for positive ions

Key points

- Most Group 1 and Group 2 metal ions can be identified using flame tests.

- Sodium hydroxide solution can be used to identify different metal ions, depending on the precipitate that is formed.

AQA Examiner's tip

Both lithium ions and calcium ions give red flame colours. Lithium ions give a brighter red but it is difficult to tell them apart from this single test. Testing solutions of the ions with sodium hydroxide solution will show which is which because calcium ions will give a white precipitate but lithium ions will not.

- Some positive ions can be identified using a flame test or by using sodium hydroxide solution.

- Some metal ions produce colours when put into a flame:

Metal ion	Flame colour
Lithium (Li^+)	crimson (red)
Sodium (Na^+)	yellow
Potassium (K^+)	lilac
Calcium (Ca^{2+})	red
Barium (Ba^{2+})	green

1 *Which metal ions give red colours in a flame?*

- The hydroxides of most metals that have ions with 2+ and 3+ charges are insoluble in water. When sodium hydroxide is added to solutions of these ions a precipitate of the metal hydroxide forms.

- Aluminium, calcium and magnesium ions form white precipitates. When excess sodium hydroxide solution is added the precipitate of aluminium hydroxide dissolves.

- Copper(II) hydroxide is blue.

- Iron(II) hydroxide is green.

- Iron(III) hydroxide is brown.

2 *A few drops of sodium hydroxide solution were added to a colourless solution and a white precipitate appeared. When excess sodium hydroxide was added the precipitate remained. Which metal ions could be present?*

Equations for the reactions of positive ions with sodium hydroxide solution

We can show the reactions of positive ions with sodium hydroxide solution by balanced ionic equations. For example:

$$Fe^{3+}(aq) + 3OH^-(aq) \rightarrow Fe(OH)_3(s)$$

Bump up your grade

If you are taking the Higher Tier paper, you should be able to write balanced symbol equations for the reactions of positive ions with sodium hydroxide solution.

Flame test colour of lithium ions

Student Book
pages 232–233 **C3**

4.2 Tests for negative ions

There are three tests for negative ions that you need to know.

- Carbonate ions: Add dilute hydrochloric acid to the substance to see if it fizzes. If it does and the gas produced turns limewater milky, the substance contains carbonate ions.

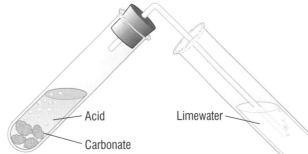

Acid

Carbonate

Limewater

The test for carbonates

E.g. $2HCl(aq) + CaCO_3(s) \rightarrow CaCl_2(aq) + H_2O(l) + CO_2(g)$

Higher

- Halide ions: Add dilute nitric acid and then silver nitrate solution:
  - chloride ions give a white precipitate
  - bromide ions give a cream precipitate
  - iodide ions give a yellow precipitate.

Precipitates of silver chloride, silver bromide and silver iodide

E.g. $AgNO_3(aq) + NaCl(aq) \rightarrow AgCl(s) + NaNO_3(aq)$

Higher

- Sulfate ions: Add dilute hydrochloric acid and then barium chloride solution. If a white precipitate forms, sulfate ions are present.

$BaCl_2(aq) + MgSO_4(aq) \rightarrow BaSO_4(s) + MgCl_2(aq)$

Higher

➤ **1** *Why must you add nitric acid and not hydrochloric acid or sulfuric acid when testing with silver nitrate solution for halides?*

Key points

- We identify carbonates by adding dilute acid, which produces carbon dioxide gas. The gas turns limewater cloudy.

- We identify halides by adding nitric acid, then silver nitrate solution. This produces a precipitate of silver halide (chloride = white, bromide = cream, iodide = pale yellow).

- We identify sulfates by adding hydrochloric acid, then barium chloride solution. This produces a white precipitate of barium sulfate.

Bump up your grade

If you are taking the Higher Tier paper, you should be able to write balanced symbol equations for the reactions in these tests.

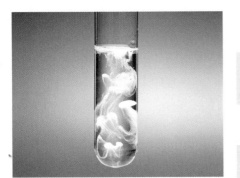

The white precipitate of barium sulfate

AQA *Examiner's tip*

Make sure you learn these tests – many candidates lose marks because they do not know the tests or their results.

4.3 Titrations

- A titration is used to measure accurately how much acid and alkali react together completely.

- The point at which an acid–base reaction is complete is called the end point of the reaction.

- We use an indicator to show the end point of the reaction between an acid and an alkali.

AQA Examiner's tip

Make sure you can describe how to use a pipette and a burette to do a titration and obtain results that are precise and repeatable.

- When solutions of an acid and an alkali react to form a salt and water, a neutralisation reaction takes place. The volumes of solutions that react exactly can be found by using a **titration**.

- To do a titration, a **pipette** is used to measure accurately the volume of alkali that is put into a conical flask. An indicator is added to the alkali. A **burette** is filled with acid, which is then added gradually to the flask.

▸ 1   What is the difference between a pipette and a burette?

- When the indicator changes colour the **end point** has been reached. The volume of acid used is found from the initial and final burette readings.

- The titration should be done several times to improve the repeatability of the results.

▸ 2   Why is an indicator needed in acid–alkali titrations?

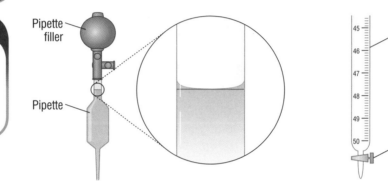

A pipette with a pipette filler attached and a burette

Titration experiment

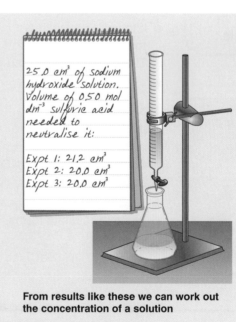

From results like these we can work out the concentration of a solution

25.0 cm³ of sodium hydroxide solution.
Volume of 0.50 mol dm⁻³ sulfuric acid needed to neutralise it:

Expt 1: 21.2 cm³
Expt 2: 20.0 cm³
Expt 3: 20.0 cm³

Key words: titration, pipette, burette, end point

Student Book
pages 236–237 **C3**

4.4 Titration calculations

Key points

- Concentrations of solutions can be measured in g/dm³ or mol/dm³.

- Concentrations can be calculated from the mass of solute dissolved in a known volume of solution.

- The mass of solute in any volume of solution can be calculated from its concentration.

- If the concentration of one of the solutions used in a titration is known, the results of the titration can be used to calculate the concentration of the other solution.

Bump up your grade

To get the highest grades in your exam, you should be able to balance symbol equations for reactions, calculate amounts of substances from titration results and apply these skills to solving problems.

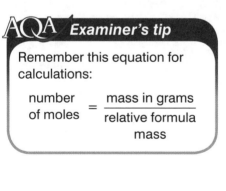

AQA Examiner's tip

Remember this equation for calculations:

$$\text{number of moles} = \frac{\text{mass in grams}}{\text{relative formula mass}}$$

Concentrations and titration calculations

- Concentrations of solutions are measured in grams per decimetre cubed (g/dm³) or moles per decimetre cubed (mol/dm³).

- If we know the mass or the number of moles of a substance dissolved in a given volume of solution we can calculate its concentration.

- If we know the volume of a solution and its concentration we can calculate the mass or the number of moles of the substance in any volume of solution.

Worked examples

a 50 cm³ of solution was made using 5.6 g of potassium hydroxide, KOH. What is its concentration in g/dm³ and mol/dm³?

1 cm³ of solution contains (5.6/50) g	so 1 dm³ of solution contains (5.6/50) × 1000 g = 112 g	concentration of solution = **112 g/dm³**
1 mole KOH = (39 + 16 + 1) g = 56 g	112 g /56 g = 2 mole	concentration of solution = **2 mol/dm³**

b What is the mass of sodium hydroxide in 100 cm³ of a solution with a concentration of 0.2 mol/dm³?

100 cm³ contains 100 × 0.2/1000 mol = 0.02 mol	1 mol NaOH = 40 g	0.02 × 40 = **8 g**

▶ **1** **100 cm³ of solution was made using 1.2 g LiOH. What is its concentration in g/dm³ and mol/dm³?**
(Relative atomic masses: Li = 7, O = 16, H = 1)

- Titrations are used to find the volumes of solutions that react exactly.

- If the concentration of one of the solutions is known, and the volumes that react together are known, the concentration of the other solution can be calculated. This information can be used to find the amount of a substance in a sample.

- The concentrations are calculated using balanced symbol equations and moles.

Worked example

A student found that 25.0 cm³ of sodium hydroxide solution with an unknown concentration reacted with exactly 20.0 cm³ of 0.50 mol/dm³ hydrochloric acid. What was the concentration of the sodium hydroxide solution?

The equation for this reaction is: NaOH(aq) + HCl(aq) → NaCl(aq) + H₂O(l)

The concentration of the HCl is 0.50 mol/dm³, so 0.50 mol of HCl are dissolved in 1000 cm³ of acid.

Therefore 20.0 cm³ of acid contains 20 × 0.50/1000 mol = 0.010 mol HCl

The equation for the reaction tells us that 0.010 mol of HCl will react with exactly 0.010 mol of NaOH.

This means that there must have been 0.010 moles of NaOH in the 25.0 cm³ of solution in the conical flask.

So, the concentration of NaOH solution = (0.010/25) × 1000 = **0.40 mol/dm³**

▶ **2** **15.0 cm³ of hydrochloric acid reacted exactly with 25.0 cm³ of sodium hydroxide solution that had a concentration of 0.10 mol/dm³. What was the concentration of the hydrochloric acid in mol/dm³?**

4.5 Chemical analysis

- Chemists and other scientists use a variety of methods to analyse substances for many purposes including environmental, medical and forensic investigations.

- They may use traditional 'wet chemistry' methods similar to those you have used in this chapter or instrumental methods such as gas chromatography and mass spectrometry (*C2 3.8*).

- Some methods, called **qualitative**, are used to find out simply if a substance is in a sample, such as the tests for ions in *C3 4.1* and *C3 4.2*. Other techniques can tell us how much of a substance is in a sample, such as titrations in *C3 4.3* and gas chromatography – mass spectrometry (GC–MS) in *C2 3.8*, and these are known as **quantitative** methods.

> **1** *When is it necessary to use quantitative analysis?*

- Large databases of the results of analyses have been built up with the aid of computers. These are used to identify substances in samples, to identify individuals, or to monitor changes in amounts of substances over time.

> **2** *Why it is necessary to have a large database for DNA analysis to be used to identify individuals?*

Key points

- Scientists working in environmental monitoring, medicine and forensic science all need to analyse substances.

- The results of their analysis are often matched against existing databases to identify substances (or suspects in the case of forensics).

Gel electrophoresis plate

Sample added | Position of bands depends on composition of DNA in sample

Analysing a DNA sample

Genetic analysis

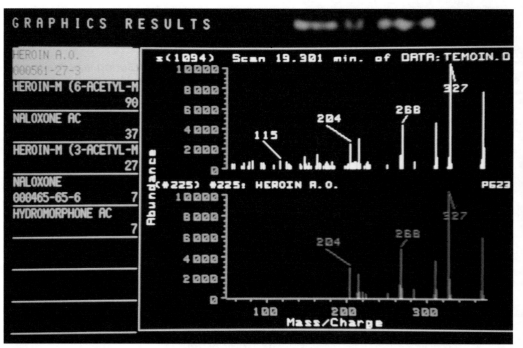

Forensic drug analysis

AQA *Examiner's tip*

In the exam you may be given results from analyses that have been done in contexts that you have not studied. Do not be put off by different contexts. Try to apply what you have learnt about the chemical tests and titrations you have done.

4.6 Chemical equilibrium

Higher

Key points

- In a reversible reaction the products of the reaction can react to re-form the original reactants. **[H]**

- In a closed system, equilibrium is achieved when the rates of the forward and reverse reactions are equal. **[H]**

- Changing the reaction conditions can change the amounts of products and reactants in a reaction mixture at equilibrium. **[H]**

AQA Examiner's tip

It is the rates of the forward and reverse reactions that are equal at equilibrium, not the amounts of reactants and products. However, the amounts of reactants and products remain constant when the reaction is at equilibrium.

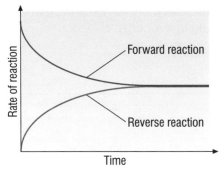

In a reversible reaction at equilibrium, the rate of the forward reaction is equal to the rate of the reverse reaction

Reversible reactions and equilibrium

Some chemical reactions are reversible. This means that the products can react together to make the reactants again:

$$A + B \rightleftharpoons C + D$$

In a closed system no reactants or products can escape. For a reversible reaction in a closed system, **equilibrium** is reached when the rate of the forward reaction is equal to the rate of the reverse reaction. At equilibrium both reactions continue to happen, but the amounts of reactants and products remain constant.

1 *Explain what is meant by equilibrium.*

Changing the concentration of a reactant or product

The amounts of the reactants and products for a reversible reaction can be changed by changing the reaction conditions. This is important for the chemical industry in controlling reactions. For example, increasing the concentration of a reactant will cause more products to be formed as the system tries to achieve equilibrium. If a product is removed, more reactants will react to try to achieve equilibrium and so more product is formed.

For example, for the reaction: $ICl + Cl_2 \rightleftharpoons ICl_3$

If chlorine is added, the concentration of chlorine is increased and more ICl_3 is produced.

If chlorine is removed, the concentration of chlorine is decreased and more ICl is produced.

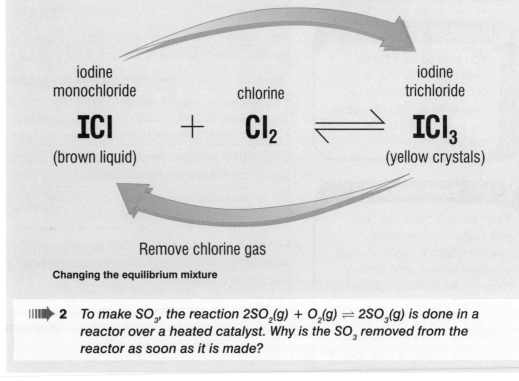

With plenty of chlorine gas

iodine monochloride | chlorine | iodine trichloride

ICl + **Cl₂** ⇌ **ICl₃**

(brown liquid) | (yellow crystals)

Remove chlorine gas

Changing the equilibrium mixture

2 *To make SO₃, the reaction $2SO_2(g) + O_2(g) \rightleftharpoons 2SO_3(g)$ is done in a reactor over a heated catalyst. Why is the SO₃ removed from the reactor as soon as it is made?*

Key word: equilibrium

4.7 Altering conditions

Key points

- Changing the pressure can affect reversible reactions involving gases at equilibrium.
  - Increasing the pressure favours the reaction with the smaller number of molecules of gas formed.
  - Decreasing the pressure favours the reaction with the larger number of molecules of gas formed.
- Changing the temperature at which we carry out a reversible reaction can change the amount of products formed at equilibrium.
  - Increasing the temperature favours the endothermic reaction.
  - Decreasing the temperature favours the exothermic reaction.

Bump up your grade

You should be able to describe the effect of changing conditions of temperature and pressure on a given reversible reaction.

AQA *Examiner's tip*

Even though there are two reactions in a reversible reaction, by convention when we write an equation for any reaction we call the substances on the left-hand side the reactants and those on the right-hand side the products.

In the exams you will be told in which direction the reaction is exothermic or endothermic.

Changing pressure

If we change the conditions of a system at equilibrium, the position of equilibrium shifts as if to try to cancel out the change.

For reversible reactions that have different numbers of molecules of gases on one side of the equation than the other, changing the pressure will affect the position of equilibrium. For example, if the pressure is increased, the position of equilibrium will shift to try to reduce the pressure (favouring the reaction that produces fewer molecules of gas).

This is summarised in the table:

If the forward reaction produces *more* molecules of gas …	If the forward reaction produces *fewer* molecules of gas …
… an increase in pressure decreases the amount of products formed.	… an increase in pressure increases the amount of products formed.
… a decrease in pressure increases the amount of products formed.	… a decrease in pressure decreases the amount of products formed.

For example: in the reversible reaction: $2NO_2(g) \rightleftharpoons N_2O_4(g)$ there are more gaseous reactant molecules than gaseous product molecules. Therefore increasing the pressure will increase the amount of N_2O_4 (product) in the mixture at equilibrium.

> **1** *For the reaction $2SO_2(g) + O_2(g) \rightleftharpoons 2SO_3(g)$, what change in pressure will increase the amount of SO_3 in the equilibrium mixture?*

Changing temperature

Reversible reactions are exothermic in one direction and endothermic in the other direction.

Increasing the temperature favours the reaction in the endothermic reaction. The equilibrium shifts as if to lower the temperature by taking in energy.

Decreasing the temperature favours the exothermic reaction.

This is summarised in the table:

If the forward reaction is exothermic …	If the forward reaction is endothermic …
… an increase in temperature decreases the amount of products formed.	… an increase in temperature increases the amount of products formed.
… a decrease in temperature increases the amount of products formed.	… a decrease in temperature decreases the amount of products formed.

For example: for the reversible reaction: $2NO_2(g) \rightleftharpoons N_2O_4(g)$ the forward reaction is exothermic, so increasing the temperature will produce more NO_2 (reactant) in the mixture at equilibrium.

> **2** *The reaction $2SO_2(g) + O_2(g) \rightleftharpoons 2SO_3(g)$ is exothermic in the forward direction. What change in temperature will increase the amount of SO_3 at equilibrium?*

Student Book
pages 244–245

C3

4.8 Making ammonia – the Haber process

Key points

- Ammonia is an important chemical for making other chemicals, including fertilisers.

- Ammonia is made from nitrogen and hydrogen in the Haber process.

- The Haber process is done using conditions which are chosen to give a reasonable yield of ammonia as quickly as possible.

- Any unreacted nitrogen and hydrogen are recycled in the Haber process.

- The Haber process is used to manufacture ammonia, which can be used to make fertilisers and other chemicals.

- Nitrogen from the air and hydrogen, which is usually obtained from natural gas, are purified and mixed in the correct proportions.

- The gases are passed over an iron catalyst at a temperature of about 450 °C and a pressure of about 200 atmospheres.

- These conditions are chosen to give a fast rate of reaction and a reasonable yield of ammonia.

- The reaction is reversible: $N_2(g) + 3H_2(g) \rightleftharpoons 2NH_3(g)$

▶ **1** *Write a word equation for the manufacture of ammonia.*

- Some of the ammonia that is produced breaks down into nitrogen and hydrogen and the yield of ammonia is only about 15%.

- The gases that come out of the reactor are cooled so the ammonia condenses. The liquid ammonia is separated from the unreacted gases. The unreacted gases are recycled so they are not wasted.

▶ **2** *What is done in the Haber process to conserve raw materials?*

Student Book
pages 246–247

C3

4.9 The economics of the Haber process

Key points

- The Haber process uses a pressure of around 200 atmospheres to increase the amount of ammonia produced.

- Although higher pressures would produce more ammonia, they would make the chemical plant too expensive to build and run.

- A temperature of about 450 °C is used for the reaction. Although lower temperatures would increase the yield of ammonia, it would be produced too slowly.

Why there is an optimum pressure for the Haber process

In the Haber process nitrogen and hydrogen react to make ammonia in a reversible reaction:

$$N_2(g) + 3H_2(g) \rightleftharpoons 2NH_3(g)$$

The products have fewer molecules of gas than the reactants, so the higher the pressure the greater the yield of ammonia. However, the higher the pressure the more energy is needed to compress the gas. Higher pressures also need stronger reaction vessels and pipes which increases costs.

A pressure of about 200 atmospheres is often used as a compromise between the costs and the yield.

▶ **1** *Why do higher pressures increase the costs of an industrial process?*

Why there is an optimum temperature for the Haber process

The forward reaction is exothermic and so the lower the temperature the greater the yield of ammonia. However, the reaction rate decreases as the temperature is lowered and the iron catalyst becomes ineffective so it would take a longer time to produce any ammonia.

Therefore, a compromise temperature of about 450 °C is usually used to give a reasonable yield in a short time.

▶ **2** *At a temperature of 100 °C and 200 atmospheres pressure the yield of ammonia is 98%. Why is the Haber process not done at this temperature?*

AQA *Examiner's tip*

Make sure you know the factors that affect the rates of reactions and understand how they apply to the Haber process.

Higher

1. When sodium hydroxide solution was added to a solution a green precipitate formed. When hydrochloric acid and barium chloride solution were added to another sample of the solution a white precipitate formed. Which ions were in the solution?

2. A compound gave a lilac colour in a flame test. Nitric acid and silver nitrate solution were added to a solution of the compound and a yellow precipitate was formed. Name the compound.

3. Dilute hydrochloric acid was added to a green compound. The mixture gave off a gas that turned limewater cloudy and a blue solution was formed. When sodium hydroxide solution was added to the blue solution a blue precipitate was produced. Name the green compound.

4. Explain how a pipette and a burette are used to do a titration.

5. Ammonia is made by the Haber process. The equation for the reaction is:
$$N_2(g) + 3H_2(g) \rightleftharpoons 2NH_3(g)$$
   a. What are the raw materials used for the process?
   b. What conditions are used in the Haber process?
   c. How is ammonia separated from the unreacted nitrogen and hydrogen?

6. $12.5\,cm^3$ of $0.10\,mol/dm^3$ hydrochloric acid reacted exactly with $25.0\,cm^3$ of potassium hydroxide solution. What was the concentration in mol/dm^3 of the potassium hydroxide solution? [H]

7. The reaction $CaCO_3(s) \rightleftharpoons CaO(s) + CO_2(g)$ reaches equilibrium in a closed system. The forward reaction is endothermic. How could the amount of calcium oxide produced by the reaction be increased? [H]

Chapter checklist	✓	✓	✓
Tick when you have:			
reviewed it after your lesson	✓	☐	☐
revised once – some questions right	✓	✓	☐
revised twice – all questions right	✓	✓	✓
Move on to another topic when you have all three ticks			

Tests for positive ions	☐	☐	☐
Tests for negative ions	☐	☐	☐
Titrations	☐	☐	☐
Titration calculations	☐	☐	☐
Chemical analysis	☐	☐	☐
Chemical equilibrium	☐	☐	☐
Altering conditions	☐	☐	☐
Making ammonia – the Haber process	■	☐	☐
The economics of the Haber process	■	☐	☐

5.1 Structures of alcohols, carboxylic acids and esters

- Organic molecules form the basis of living things and all contain carbon atoms. Carbon atoms bond covalently to each other to form the 'backbone' of many series of organic molecules.
- Series of molecules that have a general formula are called **homologous series**. The alkanes and the alkenes are two homologous series made of only hydrogen and carbon atoms.

> **1** *Name the first three members of the alkanes.*

- **Alcohols** contain the **functional group** –O–H. If one hydrogen atom from each alkane molecule is replaced with an –O–H group, we get a homologous series of alcohols.
- The first three members of this series are methanol, ethanol and propanol.

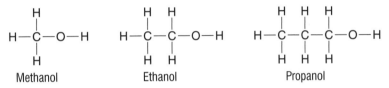

Methanol   Ethanol   Propanol

The displayed formulae of the first three members of the alcohol series

- A **structural formula** shows which atoms are bonded to each carbon atom and the functional group. The structural formula of ethanol is CH_3CH_2OH.

> **2** *Write the structural formula of propanol.*

- **Carboxylic acids** have the functional group –COOH.
- The first three members of the carboxylic acids are methanoic acid, ethanoic acid and propanoic acid. Their structural formulae are $HCOOH$, CH_3COOH and CH_3CH_2COOH.

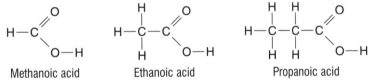

Methanoic acid   Ethanoic acid   Propanoic acid

The displayed formula of the first three carboxylic acids

> **3** *Draw the displayed formula of methanoic acid.*

- **Esters** have the functional group –COO–. If the H atom in the –COOH group of a carboxylic acid is replaced by a hydrocarbon group the compound is an ester.
- Ethyl ethanoate has the structural formula $CH_3COOCH_2CH_3$.

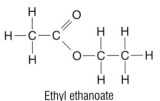

Ethyl ethanoate

The displayed formula of ethyl ethanoate

Key words: homologous series, functional group

5.2 Properties and uses of alcohols

Key points

- Alcohols are used as solvents and fuels, and ethanol is the main alcohol in alcoholic drinks.

- Alcohols burn in air, forming carbon dioxide and water.

- Alcohols react with sodium to form a solution and give off hydrogen gas.

- Ethanol can be oxidised to ethanoic acid, either by chemical oxidising agents or by the action of microbes. Ethanoic acid is the main acid in vinegar.

- Alcohols with smaller molecules, such as methanol, ethanol and propanol, mix well with water and produce neutral solutions.

- Many organic substances dissolve in alcohols and so this makes them useful solvents.

- Ethanol is the main alcohol in wine, beer and other alcoholic drinks.

> **1** *Why do many perfumes contain ethanol?*

- Alcohols burn in air. When burned completely they produce carbon dioxide and water. They are used as fuels, for example in spirit burners or in combustion engines and they can be mixed with petrol.

$$\text{ethanol} + \text{oxygen} \rightarrow \text{carbon dioxide} + \text{water}$$
$$C_2H_5OH + 3O_2 \rightarrow 2CO_2 + 3H_2O$$

- Sodium reacts with alcohols to produce hydrogen gas, but the reactions are less vigorous than when sodium reacts with water.

- Alcohols can be oxidised by chemical oxidising agents such as potassium dichromate to produce carboxylic acids. Some microbes in the air can also oxidise solutions of ethanol to produce ethanoic acid, which turns alcoholic drinks sour and is the main acid in vinegar.

> **2** *Ethanol and water are both colourless liquids. Suggest one chemical test you could do to tell them apart.*

AQA Examiner's tip

You should be able to identify the organic products of reactions from given reagents, but you do not need to be able to write balanced equations for any reactions of organic compounds, except for the combustion of alcohols.

Bump up your grade

You should know the main reactions of alcohols and how to tell if a liquid is an alcohol, an alkane, an acid or water.

Alcohols are used as solvents in perfumes

Student Book
pages 254–255

C3

5.3 Carboxylic acids and esters

Key points

- Solutions of carboxylic acids have a pH value less than 7. Their acidic solutions react with carbonates, gently fizzing as they release carbon dioxide gas.

- Aqueous solutions of weak acids have a higher pH value than solutions of strong acids with the same concentration. **[H]**

- Esters are made by reacting a carboxylic acid and an alcohol together with an acid catalyst.

- Esters are volatile compounds used in flavourings and perfumes.

Ethanoic acid reacts with carbonates to produce carbon dioxide

- Carboxylic acids dissolve in water to produce solutions with a pH value of less than 7. They have the properties typical of all acids. For example, when carboxylic acids are added to carbonates they fizz because they react to produce carbon dioxide. A salt and water are also produced.

> **1** *Why do carboxylic acids have properties similar to all other acids?*

- Carboxylic acids are different from other acids because they react with alcohols in the presence of an acid catalyst to produce esters. For example, ethanol and ethanoic acid react together when mixed with sulfuric acid as a catalyst, to produce ethyl ethanoate and water.

- Esters are volatile compounds and have distinctive smells. Some esters have pleasant fruity smells and are used as flavourings and in perfumes.

> **2** *Why are some esters used as flavourings?*

Higher

Why carboxylic acids are weak acids

- In aqueous solution, hydrochloric acid ionises completely to hydrogen ions and chloride ions.

$$HCl(aq) \rightarrow H^+(aq) + Cl^-(aq)$$

- Acids that ionise completely in aqueous solutions are known as **strong acids**.

- When ethanoic acid dissolves in water, it does not ionise completely and some of the ethanoic acid molecules remain as molecules in the solution:

$$CH_3COOH(aq) \rightleftharpoons CH_3COO^-(aq) + H^+(aq)$$

- Acids that do not ionise completely in aqueous solution are known as **weak acids**.

- In aqueous solutions of equal concentration, weak acids have a higher pH and react more slowly than strong acids.

> **3** *Write a balanced equation to show that propanoic acid is a weak acid.*

AQA *Examiner's tip*

You can tell that a solution is acidic if its pH is less than 7 or if it fizzes when added to a carbonate.

Bump up your grade

If you are taking the Higher Tier paper, you should be able to explain why carboxylic acids are weak acids and know how to tell the difference between weak and strong acids.

Key words: strong acid, weak acid

Student Book
pages 256–257

C3

5.4 Organic issues

Key points

- Alcohols, carboxylic acids and esters have many uses which benefit society.

- However, some of these substances, such as ethanol and solvents, can be abused.

- In future, the use of biofuels, such as ethanol and esters, could help society as crude oil supplies run out.

- However, future uses of biofuels might conflict with the need to feed the world.

Addiction to alcohol can cause many problems for the individuals themselves and society as a whole

- Alcohols, carboxylic acids and esters are important organic chemicals that can be used in many ways in foods, in drinks, as solvents and as fuels for the benefit of society.

- However, depending on how they are used, there can also be disadvantages. For example, alcoholic drinks and solvents can be abused and this can lead to health and social problems.

- Biofuels offer an alternative to fossil fuels and may help with the problems of diminishing resources and climate change.

- However, some of the crops used for the production of biofuels require the use of agricultural land that could be used to grow food.

- Advantages and disadvantages for any use of resources may change over time or when there are new developments and so monitoring and careful research are needed.

1 *Why is it important to review our use of organic chemicals?*

AQA *Examiner's tip*

You should have discussed some of the social and economic benefits and drawbacks of using alcohols, carboxylic acids and esters. You may be given further specific data and information in the exams.

1 Name and give the structural formula of the first three members of the series of alcohols.

2 Name and give the structural formula of the carboxylic acid with three carbon atoms in its molecule.

3 Draw the displayed formula of ethyl ethanoate.

4 What properties make ethanol a useful solvent?

5 Describe what happens when a small piece of sodium is added to some ethanol in a beaker.

6 A glass of beer containing 5% ethanol was left exposed to the air for 12 hours. The beer turned sour. Explain why.

7 Describe one reaction of ethanoic acid which is similar to the reactions of all other acids.

8 Ethanol and ethanoic acid can react together to produce an ester. Name the ester and describe the conditions used for the reaction.

9 Suggest why ethyl butanoate is added to some fruit drinks.

10 Suggest one advantage and one disadvantage of using ethanol as an alternative fuel to petrol.

11 You have been given aqueous solutions of hydrochloric acid and ethanoic acid that have the same concentration. Suggest one simple test that you could do to decide which solution is ethanoic acid. [H]

12 Write a balanced symbol equation for the complete combustion of propanol. [H]

Chapter checklist	✓ ✓ ✓

Tick when you have:				Structures of alcohols, carboxylic acids and esters	☐ ☐ ☐
reviewed it after your lesson	✓	☐	☐		
revised once – some questions right	✓	✓	☐	Properties and uses of alcohols	☐ ☐ ☐
revised twice – all questions right	✓	✓	✓		
Move on to another topic when you have all three ticks				Carboxylic acids and esters	☐ ☐ ☐
				Organic issues	☐ ☐ ☐

1 The water supplied through the mains in the UK is treated so that it is safe to drink.

a Which **two** of the following methods are used to treat mains water in the UK?
chlorination   distillation   evaporation   filtration (2 marks)

b Which **two** of the following ions cause hardness in water?
calcium   chloride   magnesium   potassium   sodium   sulfate (2 marks)

c Describe how you could test some water to find out if it is hard. Give the result of the test. (2 marks)

d When it is heated, one type of hard water produces scale.
  i What is this type of hard water called? (1 mark)
  ii Why is scale a problem? (1 mark)

e Give **two** methods that can be used to soften any type of hard water without heating. (2 marks)

f Suggest **two** reasons why mains water is not softened before it reaches the consumer. (2 marks)

g Explain, as fully as you can, how scale is formed. You should include at least **one** balanced equation in your answer. **[H]** (4 marks)

2 Methanol, ethanol and propanol are the first three members of a series of compounds.

a What general name is used for members of this series? (1 mark)

b Write the structural formula of ethanol. (1 mark)

c What is the functional group that all members of this series have? (1 mark)

d *In this question you will be assessed on using good English, organising information clearly and using specialist terms where appropriate.*

A student wanted to compare the amount of energy released when methanol, ethanol and propanol were burned. The student used the apparatus shown in the diagram.

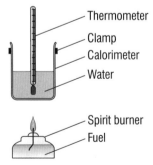

- Thermometer
- Clamp
- Calorimeter
- Water

- Spirit burner
- Fuel

The student used the equation $Q = mc\Delta T$ to calculate the energy released by each compound, with $c = 4.2$ J/g°C.

Describe how the student should use this apparatus and the measurements that he should make to compare the energy released by the three compounds. (6 marks)

e Sketch an energy level diagram for the combustion of ethanol showing the activation energy and the energy change of the reaction. (4 marks)

AQA Examiner's tip

When asked for a chemical test, as in Q1(c) and Q4, you should always describe how to do the test and give the result of the test.

AQA Examiner's tip

When you are asked for a specific number of answers, for example **two** methods in Q1(e) or **two** reasons in Q1(f) do not give more answers than the number required. If you give additional incorrect answers you will lose marks.

3 The diagram shows the Haber process for making ammonia.

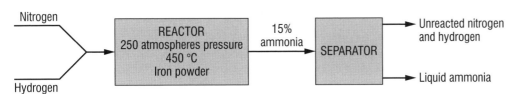

The equation for the reaction is: $N_2(g) + 3H_2(g) \rightleftharpoons 2NH_3(g)$

a What is the source of the nitrogen used in the process? *(1 mark)*

b Give **one** source of the hydrogen used in the process. *(1 mark)*

c Why is iron powder used in the reactor? *(1 mark)*

d What happens to the unreacted nitrogen and hydrogen? *(1 mark)*

e How are the conditions changed in the separator so the ammonia liquefies? *(1 mark)*

f What does the symbol $\rightleftharpoons$ tell you about the reaction? *(1 mark)*

g Explain why a high pressure is used for the reaction. **[H]** *(2 marks)*

h The yield of ammonia decreases with an increase in temperature. Explain why. **[H]** *(2 marks)*

i A relatively high temperature of 450 °C is used in the process. Explain why. **[H]** *(2 marks)*

4 For each of the following pairs of substances suggest **one** test that you could do to tell them apart. Give the results of the test for both substances.

a sodium carbonate and sodium nitrate *(2 marks)*

b potassium chloride and potassium iodide *(2 marks)*

c calcium chloride and magnesium chloride *(2 marks)*

d iron(II) sulfate and iron(III) sulfate *(2 marks)*

e ethanol and ethanoic acid *(2 marks)*

5 The table shows some bond energies. **[H]**

Bond	Bond energy in kJ per mole
C–H	413
C–C	347
O=O	498
C=O	805
H–O	464

AQA Examiner's tip

In calculations, such as in Q5, always show your working. If you make an arithmetical error, you may still gain most of the marks for correct working.

Pentane burns in air. The equation for the reaction is: $C_5H_{12} + 8O_2 \rightarrow 5CO_2 + 6H_2O$

a Use the bond energies in the table to calculate the energy change for this reaction. Show all your working. *(5 marks)*

b Explain, in terms of bond energies, why this reaction is exothermic. *(1 mark)*

Answers

C1 Answers

1 Fundamental ideas

⮕ 1.1
1 Elements
2 An atom of hydrogen
3 A compound

⮕ 1.2
1 Equal numbers of protons and electrons
2 13 protons, 13 electrons, 14 neutrons

⮕ 1.3
1 Diagram: three concentric circles with dot or Al at centre, innermost circle with 2 electrons (dots or crosses), next with 8 electrons, outer circle with 3 electrons
2 Both have 5 electrons in highest energy level (outer shell).

⮕ 1.4
1 Name of ionic compound, i.e. metal and non-metal, e.g. sodium chloride, magnesium oxide, etc.
2 Made from one calcium ion for every two chloride ions
3 It is made from three carbon atoms and eight hydrogen atoms.

⮕ 1.5
1 Magnesium reacts with hydrochloric acid to produce magnesium chloride and hydrogen; one atom of magnesium reacts with 2 molecules of hydrochloric acid to give one magnesium ion and two chloride ions and one molecule of hydrogen.
2 a $H_2 + Cl_2 \rightarrow 2HCl$
  b $4Na + O_2 \rightarrow 2Na_2O$
  c $Na_2CO_3 + 2HCl \rightarrow 2NaCl + H_2O + CO_2$ [H]

Answers to end of chapter questions
1 Elements: Ca, H_2, Ne, O_2; Compounds: CH_4, HCl, MgO, SO_2
2 11 protons, 11 electrons, 12 neutrons
3 In order of atomic numbers (proton numbers)
4 Diagram: three concentric circles with a dot or S at centre, innermost circle with 2 electrons (dots or crosses), next circle with 8 electrons, outer circle with 6 electrons
5 Both have 3 (same number of) electrons in their highest energy level (outer shell).
6 CaO ionic, C_2H_6 covalent, H_2O covalent, KCl ionic, LiCl ionic, $MgCl_2$ ionic, NH_3 covalent, Na_2O ionic, PCl_3 covalent
7 Sodium atom loses an electron and becomes a sodium ion with a positive charge, chlorine atom gains an electron and becomes a chloride ion with a negative charge.
8 a lead nitrate + potassium iodide → potassium nitrate + lead iodide
  b two potassium atoms/ions, two nitrogen atoms, six oxygen atoms, one lead atom/ion, two iodine atoms/iodide ions
9 8.8 g
10 a $2Ca + O_2 \rightarrow 2CaO$
   b $2Na + 2H_2O \rightarrow 2NaOH + H_2$
   c $CH_4 + 2O_2 \rightarrow CO_2 + 2H_2O$ [H]

2 Rocks and building materials

⮕ 2.1
1 As building blocks, to make calcium oxide, to make cement

⮕ 2.2
1 Zinc oxide and carbon dioxide
2 magnesium carbonate + hydrochloric acid → magnesium chloride + carbon dioxide + water

⮕ 2.3
1 calcium carbonate → calcium oxide + carbon dioxide
calcium oxide + water → calcium hydroxide
calcium hydroxide + carbon dioxide → calcium carbonate + water

⮕ 2.4
1 Cement is made from limestone and clay, it is used to make mortar. Mortar is cement mixed with sand and water and is used to hold bricks and blocks together. Concrete is cement mixed with sand water and aggregate (stones or crushed rock) used to make blocks, beams, buildings and roads.

⮕ 2.5
1 Advantages: More employment opportunities for local people, more customers and trade for local businesses, improved roads
Disadvantages: Dust and noise, more traffic, loss of habitats for wildlife

Answers to end of chapter questions
1 $CaCO_3$
2 By heating a mixture of limestone and clay in a kiln
3 Cement, sand, water, aggregate or crushed rock/stones
4 BreakBreaking down of a compound by heating
5 Calcium oxide and carbon dioxide
6 calcium oxide + water → calcium hydroxide
7 calcium carbonate is formed and is insoluble, calcium hydroxide + carbon dioxide → calcium carbonate + water
or $Ca(OH)_2 + CO_2 \rightarrow CaCO_3 + H_2O$
8 Acids react with calcium carbonate producing carbon dioxide and a salt. The salt dissolves in water and so the amount of limestone decreases or is worn away.
9 Calcium hydroxide reacts with acids, because calcium hydroxide is an alkali, and the reaction is neutralisation (the pH of the soil increases, which is better for growing crops).
10 $K_2CO_3 + 2HCl \rightarrow 2KCl + H_2O + CO_2$ [H]

3 Metals and their uses

⮕ 3.1
1 Rock from which metal can be extracted economically
2 a Two metals from those below carbon in the reactivity series, e.g. zinc, iron, tin, lead, copper
  b Reduction

⮕ 3.2
1 It is brittle.
2 They are harder, can be made with specific properties, can be made to resist corrosion.

⮕ 3.3
1 It requires a lot of energy for high temperatures and electricity.
2 It is strong, resists corrosion, has a low density.

⮕ 3.4
1 High-grade ores are limited or running out, to reduce environmental impacts.
2 Smelting, electrolysis, displacement

⮕ 3.5
1 Strong, good conductors of heat and electricity, can be bent and hammered into shape

2 Good conductor of electricity, can be made into wires, can be bent into shape, resistant to corrosion
3 To make it harder

⮕ 3.6
1 To save: the energy needed to extract it from its ore, resources, fossil fuels, land needed for mining and/or landfill, other specified environmental impact
2 Benefits: e.g. strong, not brittle, can be shaped, can be cut or joined or welded, cheaper than alternative metals. Drawbacks: e.g. needs protection from corrosion, heavy/dense, needs energy to extract/produce, extraction causes pollution.

Answers to end of chapter questions
1 Ore
2 It is very unreactive or very low in the reactivity series.
3 Strong, good conductors of heat and electricity, can be bent and hammered into shape.
4 Most pure metals are too soft for many uses, they need to be made harder by alloying (mixing with other elements).
5 Iron oxide is reduced by carbon when heated together. Iron oxide + carbon → iron + carbon dioxide
6 Low-carbon steel or mild steel, easily shaped; high-carbon steel, hard; stainless steel, resists corrosion
7 All steels contain iron and carbon, so are mixtures of a metal with at least one other element.
8 Three from: low density, resists corrosion, good conductor of heat and/or electricity, can be bent or hammered into shape.
9 Three from: Extraction needs several stages, uses a large amount of energy, uses a very reactive metal (for displacement), cannot be extracted using carbon
10 Three from: to save iron ore or reduce mining, to save energy or fossil fuels needed for extraction, to reduce waste going to land fill, to reduce imports of iron or iron ore
11 Phytomining and bioleaching. Phytomining uses plants to absorb copper compounds from the ground. The plants are burned and produce ash. This can be smelted to produce copper or reacted with acid to produce a solution that can be electrolysed or to which iron can be added to produce copper. Bioleaching uses bacteria to produce a solution of copper compounds that can be electrolysed or to which iron can be added to produce copper.
12 $2Fe_2O_3 + 3C \rightarrow 4Fe + 3CO_2$
$4Na + TiCl_4 \rightarrow Ti + 4NaCl$ [H]

4 Crude oil and fuels

⮕ 4.1
1 Liquids with different boiling ranges separated from a mixture of liquids (crude oil)
2 It has the general formula C_nH_{2n+2}, it is a saturated compound, it has only single carbon–carbon bonds.
3 C_4H_{10}

⮕ 4.2
1 Different hydrocarbons have different boiling points (so they condense at different levels).
2 Medium-high boiling point (about 250 °C), quite viscous/oily/thick liquid, not very flammable, burns with quite a smoky flame

4.3

1 ethane + oxygen → carbon dioxide + water
2 carbon monoxide, carbon, unburnt hydrocarbon, water
3 Acid rain

4.4

1 Particulates
2 Remove sulfur dioxide from waste gases after the fuel has been burned, remove sulfur from fuels before they are burned.

4.5

1 Biodiesel, ethanol
2 Advantage: no pollution or only product is water or can be made from water.
Disadvantage: difficult to store or production requires large amount of energy.

Answers to end of chapter questions

1 To make useful fuels/products
2 Carbon dioxide and water
3 Ignite/burn more easily, thin/runny liquids, burn with clean flame/little smoke
4 Two from: biodiesel, ethanol, hydrogen
5 Solid soot/carbon and unburnt fuel/hydrocarbons, produced by incomplete combustion
6 The fuel contains sulfur (compounds); these oxidise/burn to produce sulfur dioxide.
7 Poisonous gas carbon monoxide may be produced in limited supply of air.
8 The carbon was locked-up in fossil fuels; increases carbon dioxide in the atmosphere; carbon dioxide is a greenhouse gas; may cause global warming.
9 12 H joined to 5C, all single bonds, each C with four single bonds ($CH_3CH_2CH_2CH_2CH_3$). Four from: alkane, saturated, hydrocarbon, general formula C_nH_{2n+2}, has only single bonds, burns to produce carbon dioxide and water.
10 Crude oil vapour enters column, vapour rises, until boiling point of compound is reached, compound condenses (at that level), collected as liquid (from that level), high boiling fractions collected at bottom of column, low boiling fractions collected at top.
11 $C_2H_6O + 3O_2 → 2CO_2 + 3H_2O$ [H]
12 $2H_2 + O_2 → 2H_2O$, only product is water, no pollution, no carbon dioxide produced, can be made from water, electricity needed can be made using renewable energy source.   [H]

5 Products from oil

5.1

1 One from: to make fuels that are more useful or for which there is more demand, large hydrocarbons do not burn easily or are less in demand. memorises
2 Three from: are unsaturated, have a double bond, have a different general formula, have fewer hydrogen atoms than the corresponding alkane, are more reactive, react with or decolourise bromine water.

5.2

1 From many small molecules or monomers that react or join together or polymerise to make a very large or very long molecule
2 Thousands or a very large number
3 Alkenes are more reactive or are unsaturated or have a double bond, alkanes are unreactive or saturated or do not have a double bond.

5.3

1 A type of smart polymer or a polymer that can change to its original shape when temperature or other conditions change.

2 Two medical uses: e.g. dental fillings, removable sticking plasters, wound dressings, stitches; and two non-medical uses: e.g. packaging, waterproof fabrics, containers, bottles, clothing, fibres for duvets, water-holding composts

5.4

1 The litter would be decomposed by microorganisms when in contact with soil, and so it would not remain in the environment.
2 It can be added to plastics made from non-biodegradable polymers so they break down into small pieces; it can be used to make biodegradable plastic.

5.5

1 sugar/glucose → ethanol + carbon dioxide
2 ethene + steam → ethanol

Answers to end of chapter questions

1 Two from: to make alkenes, to make alkanes with smaller molecules, to make fuels that are more useful or for which there is more demand, large hydrocarbons do not burn easily or are less in demand, to make polymers (from alkenes)
2 By heating a mixture of hydrocarbon vapours and steam to a very high temperature, by passing hydrocarbon vapours over a hot catalyst
3 Alkanes: C_5H_{12}, C_4H_{10}, C_6H_{14} Alkenes: C_3H_6, C_4H_8
4 A polymer has very large molecules made from many small molecules called monomers joined together by a polymerisation reaction.
5 Example of use of smart polymer, e.g. shape-memory polymer used for stitching wounds
6 Can be broken down by microorganisms
7 Three from e.g. use biodegradable polymers, recycle, use plastics with cornstarch mixed in, use light-sensitive polymers, collect litter/rubbish for proper disposal.
8 By fermentation of sugar with yeast, advantages: renewable source, room temperature, disadvantages: dilute solution of ethanol, needs to be distilled to make pure ethanol, slow, batch process;
by hydration of ethene with steam and a catalyst, advantages: pure ethanol produced, continuous process, fast, disadvantages: non-renewable source, high temperature needed

9 a

NB CH_3 can be shown as H–C–H

b $C_2H_4 + H_2O → CH_3CH_2OH$ (or C_2H_5OH)   [H]
10 C_2H_4 [H]

6 Plant oils

6.1

1 (Crushing and) pressing and distillation (with water/steam)
2 They provide energy and nutrients.
3 Their molecules have carbon–carbon double bonds.

6.2

1 Cooks faster than in water, tastes better, improves the colour, better texture
2 Unsaturated oils are hydrogenated or reacted with hydrogen (at 60°C with a nickel catalyst) so they become saturated and this increases their melting points so they are solids at room temperature.   [H]

6.3

1 Opaque or not clear or cannot see through it, thick, coats solids
2 Substance that stops oil and water from separating. A substance with molecules that have a hydrophilic part and a hydrophobic part   [H]

6.4

1 Benefits (one from): high in energy, contain nutrients, contain unsaturated fats, better for health
Drawback: high in energy so easy to eat too much
2 Makes fats/oils less easily recognisable or food likely to have high fat content.

Answers to end of chapter questions

1 They provide a lot of energy.
2 Biofuel or biodiesel
3 Bromine water, turns from orange to colourless
4 Cook faster, taste better, better colour, better texture
5 Shake or stir vigorously or beat together (could also add an emulsifier).
6 Emulsifier, to prevent the oil and vinegar/water separating or to keep the emulsion stable
7 They are thicker than the oil and water they are made from, have better texture, appearance and ability to coat or stick to solids (for foods: taste better/smoother).
8 Some fats/saturated fats can cause health problems.
9 Either: crush the seeds, press the seeds, collect liquid, separate oil from water;
or: add seeds to water, boil and condense vapours/distill the mixture, collect liquids, separate oil from water
10 a React with hydrogen at 60°C with a nickel catalyst
b To harden the oils, to make the oils saturated   [H]
11 Emulsifier molecules have a hydrophilic or water-loving part (head) and a hydrophobic or water-hating part (tail). The hydrophobic part goes into oil droplets and the hydrophilic part stays at the surface keeping the droplets apart (dispersed) in the water.   [H]

7 Our changing planet

7.1

1 Core (inner), mantle, crust

7.2

1 Convection currents caused by heating of the mantle by energy from radioactivity or decay of radioactive elements
2 We do not know enough about what is happening inside the Earth or we do not have good enough data or models to make accurate predictions.
3 He could not explain why the continents moved or they had their own/different/established ideas about the Earth.

7.3

1 Volcanoes
2 Algae and plants (photosynthesis)

7.4

1 There is insufficient evidence or there are lots of theories but no proof.
2 They contain all the elements needed to make amino acids, water (H_2O) contains hydrogen and oxygen, ammonia (NH_3) contains nitrogen and hydrogen, methane (CH_4) contains carbon and hydrogen, and hydrogen is hydrogen (H_2).   [H]

7.5

1 In fossil fuels, in sedimentary rocks (including limestone)
2 78% nitrogen (almost 80%), and 21% oxygen (just over 20%)
3 It is a mixture of different substances that have different boiling points.   [H]

7.6

1 Release, two from: burning, respiration, decay; remove: photosynthesis, dissolve in oceans/water
2 Burning fossil fuels

Answers to end of chapter questions

1 Core, mantle, crust, atmosphere
2 The resources are limited.
3 Three from: carbon dioxide, water vapour, nitrogen, ammonia, methane, hydrogen
4 Four from: nitrogen, oxygen, water vapour, carbon dioxide, argon, any other named noble gas
5 When the Earth cooled water vapour condensed.
6 They removed carbon dioxide and produced oxygen.
7 a Large pieces of the Earth's crust and upper mantle
   b There are convection currents in the mantle caused by heating of the mantle by energy from radioactive decay of elements deep in the Earth.
   c A few centimetres
   d Earthquakes, volcanoes, mountains form.
8 a Natural processes maintain a balance, there is a cycle, carbon moves into and out of the atmosphere because of plants (out), animals (mainly in), oceans (in and out) and rocks (in and out).
   b Burning fossil fuels (human activity)
9 He/scientists could not explain why the continents moved. It was not until the 1960s that new evidence was discovered.
10 There is little/insufficient/conflicting evidence and many possibilities but no proof.
11 a They used a mixture of water, ammonia, methane and hydrogen and a high voltage spark to simulate lightning. This produced amino acids/organic molecules, from which proteins are made. **[H]**
   b A mixture of organic molecules/amino acids/molecules needed for life in water/oceans
12 a To separate the air into individual gases, to produce (liquid) nitrogen and oxygen (also argon), which have commercial uses or are raw materials. **[H]**
   b Air is cooled until it becomes liquid, it is put into a fractionating column, nitrogen boils at the lowest temperature or is collected as a gas or is collected at the top of the column; oxygen remains as a liquid (with argon) or is collected at the bottom of the column.

Answers to examination-style questions

1 a 15 (1 mark)
  b 15 (1 mark)
  c 16 (1 mark)
  d 5 (1 mark)
  e 5 (1 mark)
  f i phosphorus + chlorine → phosphorus chloride (1 mark)
    ii 6 (1 mark)
    iii covalent (1 mark)
2 a i calcium carbonate → calcium oxide + carbon dioxide (1 mark)
    ii Thermal decomposition (1 mark)
  b i Alkali(ne) (1 mark)
    ii Forms calcium carbonate white solid/precipitate or insoluble (2 marks)
3 a i (Fossil) fuel (1 mark)
    ii Causes acid rain or asthma or respiratory problems. (1 mark)
    iii Electrolysis (1 mark)
  b i To provide enzymes, to speed up reactions, to make copper sulfate or soluble copper compounds (1 mark)
    ii iron + copper sulfate → iron sulfate + copper (1 mark)
    iii Displacement (1 mark)

iv Two from: it is acidic or contains sulfuric acid, it contains iron salts/compounds, may contain other metal compounds, is harmful/toxic/damaging to plants/animals/humans (2 marks)
4 a high temperature catalyst or steam (2 marks)
  b Displayed formula for propene: three carbon atoms, with one single carbon–carbon bond and one double carbon–carbon bond six hydrogen atoms each with a single bond to a carbon atom so that carbon atoms all have a total of four bonds (2 marks)
  c C_2H_4 (1 mark)
  d Marks awarded for this answer will be determined by the Quality of Written Communication (QWC) as well as the standard of the scientific response.

There is a clear and detailed scientific description of the problems of plastic waste with The answer shows almost faultless spelling, punctuation and grammar. It is coherent and in an organised, logical sequence. It contains a range of appropriate and relevant specialist terms used accurately. (5–6 marks)
There is a scientific description of the problems of plastic waste. There are some errors in spelling, punctuation and grammar. The answer has some structure and organisation. The use of specialist terms has been attempted, but not always accurately. (3–4 marks)
There is a brief description of the problems of plastic waste. The spelling, punctuation and grammar are very weak. The answer is poorly organised with almost no specialist terms and/or their use demonstrating a general lack of understanding of their meaning. (1–2 marks)
No relevant content. (0 marks)

Examples of chemistry points made in the response:
Poly(propene) or poly(alkenes) or poly(ethene):
- are non-biodegradable
- cannot be broken down by microorganisms (in soil/environment)
- last for a very long time (hundreds or more years)
- large amounts used
- take up space in landfill/are bulky
- used as disposable packaging
- thrown away/become litter
- made from crude oil/use up finite resources
- difficult to identify and or separate from waste so recycling difficult
- incineration produces carbon dioxide (leading to global warming).

5 a Carbon dioxide (1 mark)
  b Water vapour/methane/ammonia/nitrogen (not oxygen) (1 mark)
  c Algae and plants (photosynthesis) (1 mark)
  d There is insufficient evidence or no proof. (1 mark)
  e Three named gases from nitrogen; **needed** [carbon dioxide; ammonia; water vapour or hydrogen that contain all four elements (C,N,H) and O) gains three marks. Three elements only or an incorrect gas (e.g. oxygen) gains two marks. Two elements only or one element missing and an incorrect gas gains one mark. **[H]** (3 marks)
  f Nitrogen (with the lowest boiling point) comes out at the top. Argon from the middle Or oxygen and argon come out at the bottom (and need further distillation to separate them). **[H]** (2 marks)

C2 Answers

1 Structure and bonding

⫸ 1.1
1 It is made of non-metals
2 KBr, Na_2O, MgO
3 Lithium atoms lose an electron to form a lithium ion that has a positive charge or Li^+; fluorine atoms gain an electron to form a fluoride ion that has a negative charge or F^-.

⫸ 1.2
1 Sodium ions have a single positive charge –they are Na^+, and magnesium ions have a double positive charge: they are Mg^{2+} (chloride ions have a single negative charge and are Cl^-)
2 Diagram of sodium atom showing one electron, chlorine atom with seven electrons, sodium ion with no electrons and positive charge, chloride ion with eight electrons and a negative charge.

⫸ 1.3
1 CaF_2, Na_2SO_4, $Mg(NO_3)_2$, $CuCl_2$, $Fe(OH)_3$

⫸ 1.4
1 Cl–Cl, H–Cl, H–S–H, O=O, O=C=O

⫸ 1.5
1 In a giant structure, closely packed together in layers with a regular pattern.
2 Electrostatic forces between positive (metal) ions and delocalised electrons.

Answers to end of chapter questions

1 A substance made of two or more elements that have reacted together or that are chemically bonded together.
2 a Outer electrons (electrons in the highest occupied energy level or outer shell).
   b They are transferred or metal atoms lose electrons and non-metal atoms gain electrons.
   c They are shared. For for each covalent bond one pair of electrons is shared.
3 a They lose their one outer electron (one electron in the highest occupied energy level or outer shell).
   b They gain one electron so their outer shell has eight electrons or so they have the structure of a noble gas.
4 H_2O, C_2H_6, CO_2,
5 The atoms in copper are all the same size, they are spherical, they are closely packed together (in a giant structure).
6 LiCl, Na_2O, CaF_2, $Mg(OH)_2$, Na_2SO_4, $Ca(NO_3)_2$
7 The attractive forces between oppositely charged ions act in all directions, so the ions pack closely together in a regular arrangement (lattice), ions are very small so a crystal contains many ions.
8 Central C with four shared pairs of electrons (o x) around it and an H outside each of the pairs of electrons.
9 F–F, O=O, H–Br, H–O–H, N with three lines each to an H
10 Diagram of a potassium atom showing one electron, fluorine atom with seven electrons, potassium ion with no electrons and positive charge, fluoride ion with eight electrons and a negative charge
11 Silicon atoms form four covalent bonds, each silicon atom can join to four others, the bonds are strong; this continues so that a giant structure is formed.
12 The outer electrons delocalise, leaving a lattice of positive ions; the delocalised electrons attract the positive ions; the electrostatic forces are strong, and these hold the ions in position. **[H]**

2 Structure and properties

⫸ 2.1
1 They have giant structures with strong electrostatic forces that hold the ions together and a lot of energy is needed to overcome the forces.
2 The ions can move freely and carry the charge.

⫸ 2.2
1 The molecules in petrol have no overall charge.
2 The intermolecular forces are greater for larger molecules. [H]

⫸ 2.3
1 Every atom is joined to several other atoms, many strong covalent bonds have to be broken and so it takes a large amount of energy to melt the giant structure.
2 Similarities: forms of carbon; giant covalent structures or covalent bonding. Differences: carbon atoms in diamond are bonded to four other carbon atoms, only to three other atoms in graphite; diamond is three-dimensional, graphite two-dimensional; diamond is hard, graphite is slippery/soft; diamond is transparent, graphite is grey/opaque; graphite is a good conductor of heat/electricity, diamond is a poor conductor; graphite has delocalised electrons, diamond does not, graphite has intermolecular forces, diamond does not.
3 Similarities: forms of carbon, hexagonal rings of atoms. Differences: graphite is a giant structure, fullerenes are molecules; graphite is two-dimensional, fullerenes are three-dimensional/cage-like; graphite forms large particles, many fullerenes are nano-sized.

⫸ 2.4
1 When stretched, the atoms slide into new positions without breaking apart.
2 They are harder than pure metals; they can be made/designed to have specific properties or special properties such as shape memory alloys.
3 Delocalised electrons move rapidly through the metal structure.

⫸ 2.5
1 They are made using different reaction conditions; they have different structures or differently shaped molecules.
2 Thermosoftening polymers have no cross-links or no covalent bonds between the polymer chains, thermosetting polymers have cross-links.
3 The weak intermolecular forces between the chains (are overcome by heating). [H]

⫸ 2.6
1 A very small particle that is a few nanometres in size, or made of a few hundreds of atoms
2 Its effects on people and the environment should be researched/tested (to ensure it is safe to use).

Answers to end of chapter questions
1 It has a giant ionic structure with strong electrostatic forces/bonds that hold the ions firmly in position and that need a lot of energy to overcome/break them.
2 They are made of small molecules or covalent bonds act only between the atoms within a molecule.
3 Different monomers change the structure of the polymer chains or the polymer chains have different shapes/structures.
4 An alloy (mixture of metals) that can be bent/deformed and changes back to its original shape when heated.
5 Every carbon atom is covalently/strongly bonded to four other carbon atoms in a giant (3-D) covalent structure.

6 The ions cannot move in the solid, but become free to move in the molten liquid or in solution.
7 The atoms are in layers. The layers slide over each other, into the new shape, without breaking apart.
8 a They are very much smaller, have a much greater surface area.
   b They are more effective (because of their greater surface area), needs to use much less silver (so it is cheaper), easier to attach to sock fibres.
9 They do not soften/melt when they get hot, they are good insulators (of heat), they can be moulded into shape but then are rigid/hard.
10 The outer electrons delocalise, leaving a lattice of positive ions; the delocalised electrons strongly attract the positive ions and hold them in position. [H]
11 There are delocalised electrons in graphite or one electron from each carbon atom is delocalised; the delocalised electrons carry the electrical charge. [H]
12 Forces between molecules (that are much weaker than covalent bonds within the molecules) [H]
13 Forms of carbon, with large molecules, based on hexagonal rings of carbon atoms, often cage-like structures, can be nano-sized, have many useful applications [H]

3 How much?

⫸ 3.1
1 The mass of an electron is very small compared to that of a proton or neutron.
2 9 protons, 9 electrons, 10 neutrons
3 Atoms of the same element or atoms with the same atomic/proton number that have different numbers of neutrons

⫸ 3.2
1 23 g
2 It has (two main) isotopes and the relative atomic mass is an average value.
3 $(23 \times 2) + 32 + (16 \times 4) = 142$
4 $24 + 12 + (16 \times 3) = 84g$ (must have g)

⫸ 3.3
1 $(12/16) \times 100 = 75\%$
2 $70/56 = 1.25 : 30/16 = 1.875$, 1:1.5, 2:3, empirical formula Fe_2O_3

⫸ 3.4
1 $CaCO_3 = 100$, $CaO = 56$, one mole $CaCO_3$ gives one mole of CaO or 100g $CaCO_3$ gives 56g CaO, 10g $CaCO_3$ gives $(10/100) \times 56 = 5.6g$

⫸ 3.5
1 $2Ca + O_2 \rightarrow 2CaO$, 80g $Ca \rightarrow$ 112g CaO, 4g $Ca \rightarrow 5.6$ g CaO, $(4.4/5.6) \times 100 = 78.6\%$
2 Reactions may not go to completion, other reactions may happen, some product may be lost when separated or collected.
3 To help conserve resources, reduce waste and/or pollution.

⫸ 3.6
1 A reaction that can go both forwards and backwards, or both ways or in both directions.

⫸ 3.7
1 Paper chromatography

⫸ 3.8
1 To separate the compounds (in the mixture)
2 From the molecular ion peak or the peak with the largest mass (furthest to the right in the spectrum)

Answers to end of chapter questions
1 a Isotopes
   b 35/17 Cl has two fewer neutrons than 37/17 Cl (18 neutrons compared with 20 neutrons).
2 Reversible

3 (Artificial) colours
4 62
5 102g
6 51.4% (51%)
7 **Two from:** magnesium oxide was lost or not collected, the magnesium did not all react, magnesium reacted with other substances in air.
8 V_2O_5 [H]
9 13.6g [H]
10 75% [H]
11 Relative molecular mass (of the compound) [H]

4 Rates and energy

⫸ 4.1
1 Amount (of reactant or product) and time
2 The gradient of the line at a given time gives the rate at that time.

⫸ 4.2
1 Activation energy
2 Increasing: temperature, concentration of solutions, pressure of gases, surface area of solids; using a catalyst
3 Powders have greater surface area than large lumps of solid, and this increases the chance of collisions.

⫸ 4.3
1 It increases the frequency of collisions and the energy of the particles.

⫸ 4.4
1 It increases the frequency of collisions.
2 The frequency of collisions increases because there are more molecules in the same volume.

⫸ 4.5
1 They remain at the end of a reaction or they are not used up in the reaction.
2 Catalysts often work with only one type of reaction.

⫸ 4.6
1 They reduce the energy needed and the time needed, and so reduce costs. They may reduce the amount of fossil fuel used and so conserve resources and reduce pollution.
2 They may be toxic or expensive.
3 Nanoscience and enzymes

⫸ 4.7
1 It transfers energy to the surroundings or heats the surroundings.
2 Either it cools the surroundings or it needs to be heated to keep it going.

⫸ 4.8
1 It is an endothermic reaction.
2 It is an exothermic reaction.

⫸ 4.9
1 One advantage e.g. less waste, less materials/resources used; one disadvantage e.g. has to be heated or needs energy so it can be used again, slower reaction, smaller temperature rise.
2 One advantage e.g. can be used anywhere, can be stored easily (ice needs to be made and/or stored in special equipment); one disadvantage e.g. can only be used once, more waste, possibly more hazardous than ice.

Answers to end of chapter questions
1 Increase concentration of acid, increase temperature, use powdered zinc, use a catalyst
2 From the gradient or slope of the line
3 The minimum energy that particles must have for collisions to produce a reaction
4 Two examples e.g. combustion, oxidation, neutralisation
5 (Thermal decomposition is) an endothermic reaction
6 High temperature, high pressure, catalyst

7 Particles are closer together (more particles in the same volume), so collisions are more frequent (more collisions per second).

8 Particles collide more frequently, and with more energy so more collisions have the activation energy (minimum energy needed for reaction).

5 Salts and electrolysis

⏵ 5.1
1 Hydrogen ions, $H^+(aq)$
2 A soluble base or a substance that produces hydroxide ions in solution, $OH^-(aq)$
3 Universal indicator or full-range indicators

⏵ 5.2
1 Any metal that is more reactive than hydrogen, but less reactive than calcium, e.g. lead, tin, iron, aluminium, magnesium.
2 To use up all of the acid or to neutralise all of the acid
3 a Magnesium nitrate and hydrogen
  b Copper chloride and water

⏵ 5.3
1 Water, H_2O
2 Zinc carbonate would be produced as a precipitate or solid, sodium sulfate would remain in the solution.

⏵ 5.4
1 They must be melted or dissolved in water.
2 a Chlorine
  b Zinc

⏵ 5.5
1 Reduction or positive sodium ions gain electrons
2 $2Cl^- \rightarrow Cl_2 + 2e^-$ [H]
3 a Oxygen
  b Copper

⏵ 5.6
1 To lower the melting temperature
2 Aluminium and carbon dioxide

⏵ 5.7
1 The solution contains hydrogen ions which are discharged in preference to sodium ions because sodium is more reactive than hydrogen.
2 Its (three) products have many uses or can be used in many ways.

⏵ 5.8
1 To make them look attractive, to protect the metal from corrosion, to reduce the cost (of making the items from pure silver).
2 Pass electricity through a cell with the item of jewellery as the negative electrode, the positive electrode made of silver and containing a solution of a silver salt (e.g. silver nitrate solution) (as the electrolyte).

Answers to end of chapter questions
1 a An alkali
  b Neutralisation
  c There is no visible change and it will show when the pH is 7.
  d nitric acid + sodium hydroxide → sodium nitrate + water
2 Add zinc oxide, a little at a time, to dilute sulfuric acid, until there is an excess, filter off the excess, evaporate some of the water, leave to cool and crystallise.
3 Mix the two solutions, filter the mixture or leave to settle and decant or centrifuge and decant to separate the solid (precipitate). Then wash with distilled water and dry.
4 Less expensive than pure gold, to improve appearance, so they do not corrode (or cause allergic reactions)
5 Hydrogen, chlorine and sodium hydroxide. A use for each, e.g. hydrogen: to make hydrochloric

acid, margarine manufacture, fuel; chlorine: to make bleach, plastics; sodium hydroxide: to make soap, paper, as a cleaning agent (ovens/drains)
6 a It needs: large amounts of electricity, high temperature to melt the aluminium oxide.
  b To lower the melting/operating temperature (of the electrolyte)
7 At the negative electrode: sodium ions gain electrons, are reduced, to sodium atoms/metal. At the positive electrode: chloride ions lose electrons, are oxidised, to chlorine atoms, which form chlorine molecules/gas.
8 At the negative electrode: $2H^+ + 2e^- \rightarrow H_2$
  At the positive electrode: $2Cl^- \rightarrow Cl_2 + 2e^-$ [H]

Answers to examination-style questions

1 a Li – metallic, F_2 – covalent, LiF – ionic
    (3 marks)
  b F_2 (1 mark)
  c i Li
    ii Li and LiF   (2 marks)
  d i

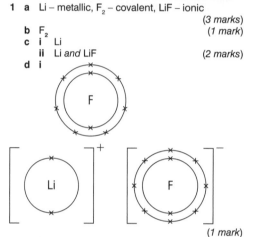

    (1 mark)
    ii Li at centre of one circle with two crosses with brackets and + sign top right outside bracket
      F at centre of two concentric circles with two crosses on inner circle and eight crosses on outer circle enclosed in brackets with – sign top right outside brackets   (4 marks)
  e i A particle that is a few nm (nanometres) in size or containing a few hundred atoms   (1 mark)
    ii Much larger surface area, react much faster or more easily, or other different property   (1 mark)
  f The electrons in the highest energy level (outer shell)
    are delocalised
    and attract or hold the positive metal ions together
    by strong electrostatic forces   [H] (4 marks)
2 a 136 (no units)   (2 marks)
    if incorrect: $40 + 1 + 31 + (4 \times 16)$ gains 1 mark
  b 29.4%   (2 marks)
    allow error carried forward from a; if answer incorrect: correct working (40/136) or answer to a ×100 gains 1 mark
  c $CaCO_3$ contains more
    Working: either $(40/100) \times 100\% = 40\%$ Ca or CO_3 (60) < HPO_4 (96)   (2 marks)
  d Isotopes are atoms of the same element or atoms with the same number of protons with different numbers of neutrons or different mass numbers
    $^{31}_{15}P$ has 16 neutrons, $^{32}_{15}P$ has 17 neutrons   (3 marks)
  e Mass in 100g = 43.7g P : 56.3g O
    Moles of atoms = 43.7/31 : 56.3/16 (divide by A_r)

Ratio of atoms = 1.41 : 3.52
Divide by 1.41 = 1 : 2.5
Simplest ratio = 2 : 5, so empirical formula is P_2O_5 (4 marks)
3 a It is reversible.   (1 mark)
  b N with 3H at least 90° apart, with xo between each H and N (1) and xx close to N giving a total of 8 electrons around N   (2 marks)

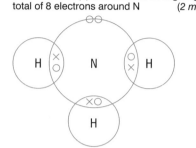

  c It produces $OH^-(aq)$.   (1 mark)
  d i $H^+(aq) + OH^-(aq) \rightarrow H_2O(l)$ (1 mark)
    ii Neutralisation   (1 mark)
    iii Marks awarded for this answer will be determined by the standard of the scientific response as well as the Quality of Written Communication (QWC).
      There is a clear, logical and detailed scientific description of how to make ammonium nitrate crystals including an appropriate risk assessment. The answer shows almost faultless spelling, punctuation and grammar. It is coherent and in an organised, logical sequence. It contains a range of appropriate and relevant specialist terms used accurately.   (5–6 marks)
      There is a scientific description of how to make ammonium nitrate crystals and an attempt at risk assessment. There are some errors in spelling, punctuation and grammar. The answer has some structure and organisation. The use of specialist terms has been attempted, but not always accurately.   (3–4 marks)
      There is a brief description of how to make ammonium nitrate but a risk assessment may be missing. The spelling, punctuation and grammar are very weak. The answer is poorly organised with almost no specialist terms and/or their use demonstrating a general lack of understanding of their meaning.   (1–2 marks)
      No relevant content.   (0 marks)

Examples of chemistry points made in the candidate's response:
  • Use UI paper or use pH meter/probe to check pH
  • Add ammonia solution to dilute nitric acid
  • A little at a time
  • Stir or swirl the mixture
  • Until indicator changes colour or until excess ammonia or ammonia can be smelled
  • Remove indicator (boil with charcoal and filter)
  • Heat solution to evaporate some water (and excess ammonia)
  • Allow solution to cool and crystallise (allow to evaporate slowly)
  • Separate crystals from any remaining solution
  • Dilute nitric acid is irritant/corrosive – risk to eyes and skin etc
  • Ammonia solution is irritant/corrosive – risk to eyes and skin etc.
  • Heating/evaporating solution – risk to eyes and skin etc.
  • Wear safety goggles, wipe up spillages, avoid contact with skin and clothes, care when heating.

e i Relative formula masses:
$NH_3 = 17$, $NH_4NO_3 = 80$
Number of moles $NH_3 = 1.7/17 = 0.1$
From equation, number of moles of $NH_3 =$
number of moles of NH_4NO_3 or 17 g NH_3
produces 80 g NH_4NO_3
Mass of 0.1 mole $NH_4NO_3 = 80 \times 0.1 =$
8 g or 1.7 g NH_3 produces 8 g NH_4NO_3
[H] (3 marks)

ii $(5.2/8.0) \times 100$
= 65% [H] (2 marks)
(1 mark)

4 a Exothermic
b A substance that speeds up a reaction without being used up in the reaction (2 marks)
c Two from: increase the surface area of iron or use smaller particles/nanoparticles of iron, increase the concentration of salt, increase flow of air e.g. shake or blow on the pack (2 marks)

5 a Chlorine (1 mark)
b Hydrogen (1 mark)
c Sodium hydroxide (1 mark)
d Sodium is more reactive than hydrogen so hydrogen ions are discharged in preference to sodium ions. (2 marks)
e $2Cl^-(aq) \rightarrow Cl_2(g) + 2e^-$
because chloride ions lose electrons or oxidation is loss of electrons. [H] (2 marks)

C3 Answers

1 The periodic table

1.1
1 Protons (and electrons) had not been discovered or they did not know about atomic structure.
2 The elements fitted better into the groups (because he had left gaps).

1.2
1 They have the same number of electrons in the highest occupied energy level or outer shell.
2 When metals react their atoms lose electrons, as the atoms get larger there are more occupied energy levels and the electrons in the highest occupied level or outer shell are less strongly attracted by the nucleus and so are lost more easily.

1.3
1 They react with water to produce alkalis or their hydroxides are alkalis.
2 Potassium bromide, KBr
3 Lithium atoms are smaller than sodium atoms, they have fewer occupied energy levels (Li 2,1; Na 2,8,1), their outer electron is more strongly attracted by the nucleus, and so is less easily lost when they react (to form an ion).

1.4
1 They are strong, hard, react only slowly (or not at all) with oxygen/air and water (at ordinary temperatures).
2 Higher melting points, stronger, harder, denser, less reactive (with oxygen and water), ions have different charges, coloured compounds, catalysts.

1.5
1 They have small molecules (made of pairs of atoms).
2 Add chlorine (water) to a solution of potassium bromide (or other soluble bromide), bromine will be displaced.

Answers to end of chapter questions
1 When the elements are arranged in order of atomic weights, every eighth element has similar properties.

2 The elements fitted the groups better or the elements within a group all had similar properties, it allowed for undiscovered elements or left gaps for undiscovered elements.
3 They have the same number of electrons in the highest occupied energy level or outer shell (same number of outer electrons).
4 a lithium + water → lithium hydroxide + hydrogen
b Three from: lithium floats, moves around the surface, gradually disappears, bubbles (of gas) or fizzes.
c Add (universal) indicator, goes purple or blue (or correct alkaline colour for named indicator).
d Sodium reacts faster or melts (lithium does not melt).
5 Physical: (three from) high melting point (and/or boiling point), hard, strong, high density, malleable, ductile, good conductor (of heat and electricity), can be made into alloys. Chemical: (three from) unreactive or reacts slowly with oxygen (air) and/or water, forms positive ions/ionic compounds, forms ions with different charges, coloured compounds, catalyst.
6 They increase.
7 NaBr; colourless or white, crystals or solid; dissolves in water, forms a colourless solution.
8 Covalently bonded, small molecules (has weak forces between its molecules).
9 a From colourless to orange/yellow/brown.
b chlorine + potassium bromide → potassium chloride + bromine
c $Cl_2 + 2KBr \rightarrow 2KCl + Br_2$ [H]
10 $2Fe + 3Cl_2 \rightarrow 2FeCl_3$ [H]
11 a A sodium atom has more occupied energy levels/shells, so its outer electron is further from and less strongly held by the nucleus, and so can be more easily lost when it reacts.
b A fluorine atom has fewer occupied energy levels/shells, so its nucleus has a greater attraction for electrons in the highest occupied energy level/outer shell, so it attracts electrons more readily when it reacts. [H]

2 Water

2.1
1 Soft water lathers easily with only a little soap, hard water uses more soap and produces scum.
2 Scum is formed when soap reacts with compounds in hard water. Scale is produced when temporary hard water is heated or boiled.
3 Hard water contains calcium compounds that are good for health, for the development of teeth and bones, and to reduce the risk of heart disease.

2.2
1 Water that is softened by heating or boiling, (and forms scale when heated).
2 $Ca^{2+}(aq) + CO_3^{2-}(aq) \rightarrow CaCO_3(s)$ [H]
3 Ion-exchange resin removes the calcium and magnesium ions from hard water and replaces them (exchanges them) for sodium ions or hydrogen ions (that do not react with soap).

2.3
1 Sedimentation and/or filtration to remove solids, killing microbes (disinfecting/sterilising) using chlorine (or other methods, e.g. ozone, ultraviolet).
2 It requires a large amount of energy and so it would be very expensive and/or tap water does not need to be pure but should be free from harmful substances.

2.4
1 Advantage: (one of) uses less soap, does not produce scum, reduces the effects on heating systems. Disadvantage (one of): reduces health benefits, costs money.
2 No chlorine: increased health risks, more (water-borne) spreading of disease. No fluoride: more tooth decay or poorer dental health.

Answers to end of chapter questions
1 Soap reacts with calcium and/or magnesium ions/compounds to produce insoluble solids.
2 Scale (insoluble solids of calcium carbonate and magnesium carbonate)
3 Health benefit, e.g. stronger teeth and bones or reduced risk of heart attacks
4 Temporary hard water is softened or produces scale when heated/boiled, permanent hard water is not softened or does not produce scale when heated/boiled.
5 Washing soda is sodium carbonate which is soluble, calcium ions and/or magnesium ions in the water react with carbonate ions to produce precipitates/insoluble calcium carbonate and/or magnesium carbonate, thus removing the ions from the water so they cannot react with soap.
6 It replaces calcium ions with sodium ions that can have negative health effects or increase the risk of heart disease.
7 Insoluble solids
8 To kill microbes/bacteria (to disinfect or sterilise the water).
9 No need for drinking water to be pure water or drinking water just needs to be free from harmful substances.
10 To reduce the amount of tooth decay or to improve dental health.
11 Hydrogencarbonate ions decompose when heated to produce carbonate ions, water and carbon dioxide:
$2HCO_3^-(aq) \rightarrow CO_3^{2-}(aq) + H_2O(l) + CO_2(g)$
Carbonate ions react with calcium ions and/or magnesium ions in the water to produce precipitates of calcium carbonate and/or magnesium carbonate that are deposited as scale:
$Ca^{2+}(aq) + CO_3^{2-}(aq) \rightarrow CaCO_3(s)$ or
$Mg^{2+}(aq) + CO_3^{2-}(aq) \rightarrow MgCO_3(s)$ [H]

3 Energy calculations

3.1
1 36 400 J or 36.4 kJ
2 Fuel B (A releases 2620.8 kJ/mol and B releases 4058.4 kJ/mol)

3.2
1 7560 J or 7.56 kJ
2 142.8 kJ/mol of iron

3.3
1 Energy level diagram similar to figure but with the products at a higher energy level than the reactants.
2 Energy level diagram similar to figure but with the products at a higher level than the reactants, the reaction pathway rising above the products level, and the activation energy labelled with an arrow pointing upwards from the reactants level to the top of the pathway curve.
3 Energy level diagram similar to figure but with the products at a higher level than the reactants. The catalysed pathway should be labelled and its peak should be below the peak for the uncatalysed pathway (i.e. has a lower activation energy).

⫸ 3.4

1 Bonds broken: $(2 \times$ C–C$) + (8 \times$ C–H$) + (5 \times$ O=O$)$, energy needed = 6488kJ,
Bonds made: $6 \times$ C=O $+ 8 \times$ H–O = 8542kJ
Energy change of reaction = 2054 kJ/mol   [H]

⫸ 3.5

1 Fossil fuels are non-renewable or a limited resource, fossil fuels cause pollution or release carbon dioxide that causes global warming, hydrogen produces only water or does not produce carbon dioxide or other pollutants, hydrogen releases a large amount of energy per gram, hydrogen can be produced from renewable sources.

Answers to end of chapter questions

1 Energy losses or it is not only the water that is heated.
2 The energy level of the reactants is below the level of the products.
3 Diagram similar to third figure in C3 3.3, with reactants on line above products, reaction pathway shown as curved line reaching maximum above reactants, activation energy shown as an arrow from reactants to maximum of pathway and energy change of reaction shown as arrow pointing downwards from reactants to products.
4 12600J or 12.6kJ (or 25.2kJ/g)
5 75.6 kJ/mol
6 58.8 kJ/mol
7 Diagram similar to third figure in C3 3.3, with reactants on line above products and two reaction pathways, the one with the lower maximum labelled 'with catalyst'.
8 Three from: supply, storage, safety, performance, convenience, price/cost of vehicles
9 542 kJ/mol   [H]
10 1318 kJ/mol   [H]

4 Analysis and synthesis

⫸ 4.1

1 Lithium (Li^+) and calcium (Ca^{2+})
2 Calcium (Ca^{2+}) and magnesium (Mg^{2+})

⫸ 4.2

1 Hydrochloric acid contains chloride ions (Cl^-) and sulfuric acid contains sulfate ions (SO_4^{2-}) which both give precipitates with silver nitrate solution.

⫸ 4.3

1 A pipette measures a fixed volume, has a single graduation, and has no tap; a burette measures different volumes, has graduations, has a tap.
2 To show when the end-point is reached or when the reaction is complete or when the acid and alkali have reacted exactly.

⫸ 4.4

1 12g/dm³, 0.5mol/dm³   [H]
2 0.17mol/dm³   [H]

⫸ 4.5

1 When we need to know how much or the quantity of a substance in a sample.
2 DNA results/profile are different for every individual.

⫸ 4.6

1 When the rates of the forward and reverse reactions of a reversible reaction are equal or when the amounts of reactants and products in a reversible reaction are constant.   [H]
2 So that more of the reactants react or so more SO_3 is produced.   [H]

⫸ 4.7

1 An increase in pressure
2 A decrease in temperature

⫸ 4.8

1 nitrogen + hydrogen ⇌ ammonia
2 Unreacted gases are recycled.

⫸ 4.9

1 More energy is needed and stronger reaction vessels and pipes are needed which both cost more.   [H]
2 The reaction would be too slow (rate decreased and catalyst will not work)   [H]

Answers to end of chapter questions

1 Fe^{2+}/iron(II) ions and SO_4^{2-}/sulphate ions
2 Potassium iodide (KI)
3 Copper(II) carbonate ($CuCO_3$)
4 A pipette is used to measure a fixed volume (e.g. 25 cm³) of (alkali) solution (into a conical flask). A burette is used to add (acid) solution (gradually) to the flask until the end-point of the reaction is reached and to measure the volume that has been added.
5 a Air (nitrogen), natural gas (hydrogen)
  b About 200 atmospheres pressure, about 450°C, iron catalyst.
  c The gases are cooled (as they leave the reactor) and ammonia condenses (liquefies) but nitrogen and hydrogen remain as gases.
6 0.05mol/dm³   [H]
7 By increasing the temperature, by removing carbon dioxide or allowing it to escape.   [H]

5 Organic chemistry

5.1

1 methane, ethane and propane
2 $CH_3CH_2CH_2OH$
3 Displayed formula of HCOOH

5.2

1 It is a solvent (it mixes with water, it evaporates easily)
2 One of: apply a flame – ethanol burns in air: add sodium – ethanol reacts more slowly (also sinks in ethanol): add (acidified) potassium dichromate (or other oxidising agent) and heat – colour change or smell of vinegar

5.3

1 They produce H^+(aq), hydrogen ions in aqueous solutions.
2 They have distinctive smells/tastes that are fruity/pleasant.
3 CH_3CH_2COOH(aq) ⇌ $CH_3CH_2COO^-$ (aq) + H^+(aq)   [H]

5.4

1 Advantages and disadvantages may change over time as resources are used up or there are new developments or new research.

Answers to end of chapter questions

1 Methanol, ethanol and propanol, CH_3OH, CH_3CH_2OH, $CH_3CH_2CH_2OH$
2 Propanoic acid, CH_3CH_2COOH
3

Ethyl ethanoate
4 Dissolves many substances, mixes with water, evaporates easily (volatile).
5 It reacts, fizzes/effervesces, produces hydrogen (slower than with water, sodium sinks)
6 Microbes in the air, caused oxidation of ethanol, produced ethanoic acid.

7 Reacts with carbonates to produce carbon dioxide (and a salt and water) or reacts with metals to produce hydrogen and a salt, or reacts with bases/alkalis to produce a salt and water.
8 Ethyl ethanoate, (sulfuric) acid catalyst, heat the mixture.
9 It is an ester and so has a fruity smell/flavour.
10 One advantage, e.g. can be produced from renewable resources, does not release locked-up carbon or is carbon neutral; one disadvantage, e.g. need food crops/land for production.
11 Test with universal indicator or pH meter/probe, ethanoic acid has higher pH: or add a metal or carbonate, ethanoic acid reacts slower.   [H]
12 $CH_3CH_2CH_2OH + 4.5O_2 \rightarrow 3CO_2 + 4H_2O$ or $2CH_3CH_2CH_2OH + 9O_2 \rightarrow 6CO_2 + 8H_2O$ [H]

Answers to examination-style questions

1 a chlorination, filtration   (2 marks)
  b calcium, magnesium   (2 marks)
  c add soap solution and shake, scum forms or does not lather   (2 marks)
  d i temporary hard water   (1 mark)
    ii reduces efficiency of water heating systems, blocks pipes   (1 mark)
  e add sodium carbonate (washing soda), use ion exchange column/resin   (2 marks)
  f Two from: too expensive, no need to soften all water supplied, hard water is better for health, water only needs to be safe to drink, choice left to consumer.   (2 marks)
  g Four from: Temporary hard water contains hydrogencarbonate ions (HCO_3^-), these decompose on heating producing carbonate ions, $2HCO_3^- \rightarrow CO_2 + CO_3^{2-} + H_2O$, carbonate ions react with calcium and magnesium ions to form precipitates (removing the ions from solution), $Ca^{2+} + CO_3^{2-} \rightarrow CaCO_3$ or $Mg^{2+} + CO_3^{2-} \rightarrow MgCO_3$.   [H] (4 marks)
2 a alcohols   (1 mark)
  b CH_3CH_2OH (1 mark)
  c –OH   (1 mark)
  d Marks awarded for this answer will be determined by the Quality of Written Communication (QWC) as well as the standard of the scientific response.

  There is a clear and detailed description showing the detailed understanding of the method. Knowledge of accurate information appropriately contextualised. The answer shows almost faultless spelling, punctuation and grammar. It is coherent and in an organised, logical sequence. It contains a range of appropriate and relevant specialist terms used accurately.   (5–6 marks)
  There is some description showing a clear understanding of the method. There are some errors in spelling, punctuation and grammar. The answer has some structure and organisation, use of specialist terms has been attempted but not always accurately.   (3–4 marks)
  There is a brief description of the method. The spelling, punctuation and grammar are very weak. The answer is poorly organised, with almost no specialist terms and their use demonstrates a general lack of understanding of their meaning.   (1–2 marks)
  No relevant content.   (0 marks)

Examples of chemistry points made in the candidate's response:

- Measure appropriate volume of water in measuring cylinder and put into into calorimeter.
- Measure the initial temperature.
- Measure the mass of the spirit burner.
- Ignite spirit burner and place under calorimeter. Allow to burn until suitable temp rise or for a few minutes. Put out flame. Stir water.
- Record the highest steady temperature.
- Re-weigh spirit burner.
- Calculate temperature change.
- Calculate mass of compound burned.
- Assume volume water (cm^3) = mass of water (g). Calculate energy change for 1 g (or 1 mole) of each fuel to compare.
- Evidence of high level work e.g. appropriate quantities, use of precise balance, appropriate size of measuring cylinder, attempt to reduce draughts, e.g. use of shields, using same sized flame, same distance from calorimeter base.

e One mark for each of the following:
Energy level diagram with reactants (labelled) above level of products
curve showing energy change during reaction that peaks above reactants
activation energy labelled as arrow from level with reactants to maximum of curve
energy change of reaction labelled as arrow from level with reactants to level with products. *(4 marks)*

3 a The air *(1 mark)*
b e.g. natural gas, crude oil/naphtha/product of cracking hydrocarbons, (allow electrolysis of water or brine – not usually used but are possible sources). *(1 mark)*
c Catalyst or to speed up the reaction. *(1 mark)*
d recycled or returned to the reactor *(1 mark)*
e cooled or temperature decreased *(1 mark)*
f reversible reaction *(1 mark)*
g There are four molecules (moles) of reactant gases and two molecules of product gases or fewer molecules of gas in products than reactants (1) so high pressure favours forward reaction. **[H]** *(2 marks)*
h The forward reaction is exothermic or reverse reaction is endothermic (1) high temperature favours the endothermic reaction or the reverse reaction or low temperature favours the exothermic reaction (1) **[H]** *(2 marks)*
i The rate of reaction is higher at higher temperatures (1)
so ammonia is produced quickly (1)
or
converse argument gains 2 marks or the catalyst only works at high temperatures gains 1 mark. **[H]** *(2 marks)*
4 a add hydrochloric acid (or other named acid)
carbonate effervesces/fizzes or produces carbon dioxide gas, nitrate has no reaction. *(2 marks)*
b Add dilute nitric acid and silver nitrate solution
white precipitate with chloride, yellow precipitate with iodide. *(2 marks)*

c Flame test
calcium chloride gives red flame colour, magnesium chloride gives no colour *(2 marks)*
d Add sodium hydroxide solution
green precipitate with iron(III) sulfate and brown precipitate with iron(III) sulfate. *(2 marks)*
e Test pH of aqueous solution using named indicator or pH meter/probe
ethanol solution pH 7 or appropriate neutral colour of indicator (e.g. UI green) and ethanoic acid pH < 7 or appropriate acid colour of indicator (e.g. UI red) **[H]** *(2 marks)*
5 a Bonds broken: $4 \times$ C–C + $12 \times$ C–H + $8 \times$ O=O = 10328
Bonds made: $10 \times$ C=O + $12 \times$ C–H = 13618
Energy change = 3290 kJ *(5 marks)*
b Energy released when bonds made (in products) is greater than energy needed to break bonds (in reactants) *(1 mark)*

Glossary

A

Acid A sour substance that can attack metal, clothing or skin. The chemical opposite of an alkali. When dissolved in water, its solution has a pH number less than 7. Acids are proton (H+ ion) donors.

Activation energy The minimum energy needed to start off a reaction.

Alkali metal Elements in Group 1 of the periodic table, e.g. lithium (Li), sodium (Na), potassium (K).

Alkali Its solution has a pH number more than 7.

Alkane Saturated hydrocarbon with the general formula C_nH_{2n+2}, for example methane, ethane and propane.

Alkene Unsaturated hydrocarbon which contains a carbon–carbon double bond. The general formula is C_nH_{2n}, for example ethene C_2H_4.

Alloy A mixture of metals (and sometimes non-metals). For example, brass is a mixture of copper and zinc.

Aluminium A low density, corrosion-resistant metal used in many alloys, including those used in the aircraft industry.

Anhydrous Describes a substance that does not contain water.

Aqueous solution The mixture made by adding a soluble substance to water.

Atmosphere The relatively thin layer of gases that surround planet Earth.

Atom The smallest part of an element that can still be recognised as that element.

Atomic number The number of protons (which equals the number of electrons) in an atom. It is sometimes called the proton number.

Atomic weight The historical term that was used before relative atomic masses were defined in the 20th century. See Relative atomic mass, A_r.

B

Base The oxide, hydroxide or carbonate of a metal that will react with an acid, forming a salt as one of the products. (If a base dissolves in water it is called an alkali). Bases are proton (H+ ion) acceptors.

Biodegradable Materials that can be broken down by microorganisms.

Biodiesel Fuel for cars made from plant oils.

Biofuel Fuel made from animal or plant products.

Bioleaching Process of extraction of metals from ores using microorganisms.

Blast furnace The huge reaction vessels used in industry to extract iron from its ore.

Bond energy The energy needed to break a particular chemical bond.

Burette A long glass tube with a tap at one end and markings to show volumes of liquid, used to add precisely known amounts of liquids to a solution in a conical flask below it.

C

Calcium carbonate The main compound found in limestone. It is a white solid whose formula is $CaCO_3$.

Calcium hydroxide A white solid made by reacting calcium oxide with water. It is used as a cheap alkali in industry.

Calcium oxide A white solid made by heating limestone strongly, for example, in a lime kiln.

Carbon monoxide A toxic gas whose formula is CO.

Cast iron The impure iron taken directly from a blast furnace.

Catalyst A substance that speeds up a chemical reaction. At the end of the reaction the catalyst remains chemically unchanged.

Cement A building material made by heating limestone and clay.

Chromatography The process whereby small amounts of dissolved substances are separated by running a solvent along a material such as absorbent paper.

Collision theory An explanation of chemical reactions in terms of reacting particles colliding with sufficient energy for a reaction to take place.

Compound A substance made when two or more elements are chemically bonded together. For example, water (H_2O) is a compound made from hydrogen and oxygen.

Concrete A building material made by mixing cement, sand and aggregate (crushed rock) with water.

C

Convection current The circular motion of matter caused by heating in fluids.

Copper-rich ore Rock that contains a high proportion of a copper compound.

Core The centre of the Earth.

Covalent bonding The attraction between two atoms that share one or more pairs of electrons.

Cracking The reaction used in the oil industry to break down large hydrocarbons into smaller, more useful ones. This occurs when the hydrocarbon vapour is either passed over a hot catalyst or mixed with steam and heated to a high temperature.

Crust The outer solid layer of the Earth.

D

Delocalised electron Bonding electron that is no longer associated with any one particular atom.

Displace When one element takes the place of another in a compound. For example, iron + copper sulfate → iron sulfate + copper.

Distillation Separation of a liquid from a mixture by evaporation followed by condensation.

Dot and cross diagram A drawing to show the arrangement of the outer shell electrons only of the atoms or ions in a substance.

Double bond A covalent bond made by the sharing of two pairs of electrons.

E

Electrolyte A liquid, containing free-moving ions, that is broken down by electricity in the process of electrolysis.

Electron A tiny particle with a negative charge. Electrons orbit the nucleus in atoms or ions.

Electronic structure A set of numbers to show the arrangement of electrons in their shells (or energy levels), for example, the electronic structure of a potassium atom is 2, 8, 8, 1.

Element A substance made up of only one type of atom. An element cannot be broken down chemically into any simpler substance.

Empirical formula The simplest ratio of elements in a compound.

Emulsifier A substance which helps keep immiscible liquids (for example, oil and water) mixed so that they do not separate out into layers.

Emulsion A mixture of liquids that do not dissolve in each other.

End point The point in a titration where the reaction is complete and titration should stop.

Endothermic A reaction that *takes in* energy from the surroundings.

Energy level see Shell.

Equilibrium The point in a reversible reaction in which the forward and backward rates of reaction are the same. Therefore, the amounts of substances present in the reacting mixture remain constant.

Ethene An alkene with the formula C_2H_4.

Exothermic A reaction that *gives out* energy to the surroundings.

F

Fermentation The reaction in which the enzymes in yeast turn glucose into ethanol and carbon dioxide.

Flammable Easily ignited and capable of burning rapidly.

Fraction Hydrocarbons with similar boiling points separated from crude oil.

Fractional distillation A way to separate liquids from a mixture of liquids by boiling off the substances at different temperatures, then condensing and collecting the liquids.

Fullerene Form of the element carbon that can form a large cage-like structure, based on hexagonal rings of carbon atoms.

Functional group An atom or group of atoms that give organic compounds their characteristic reactions.

G

Gas chromatography The process of separating the components in a mixture by passing the vapours through a column and detecting them as they leave the column at different times.

Giant covalent structure A huge 3-D network of covalently bonded atoms (e.g. the giant lattice of carbon atoms in diamond or graphite).

Giant lattice A huge 3-D network of atoms or ions (e.g. the giant ionic lattice in sodium chloride).

Giant structure See giant lattice.

Global dimming The reflection of sunlight by tiny solid particles in the air.

Global warming The increasing of the average temperature of the Earth.

Gradient Change of the quantity plotted on the *y*-axis divided by the change of the quantity plotted on the *x*-axis.

Group All the elements in each column (labelled 1 to 7 and 0) down the periodic table.

H

Hard water Water in which it is difficult to form a lather with soap. It contains calcium and/or magnesium ions which react with soap to produce scum.

Hardening The process of reacting plant oils with hydrogen to raise their melting point. This is used to make spreadable margarine.

Homologous series A group of related organic compounds that have the same functional group, e.g. the molecules of the homologous series of alcohols all contain the –OH group.

Hydrated Describes a substance that contains water in its crystals, e.g. hydrated copper sulfate.

Hydrocarbon A compound containing only hydrogen and carbon.

Hydrogenated oil Oil which has had hydrogen added to reduce the degree of saturation in the hardening process to make margarine.

Hydrophilic The water-loving part of an emulsifier molecule.

Hydrophobic The water-hating hydrocarbon part of an emulsifier molecule.

I

Incomplete combustion When a fuel burns in insufficient oxygen, producing carbon monoxide as a toxic product.

Inert Unreactive.

Intermolecular force The attraction between the individual molecules in a covalently bonded substance.

Ion A charged particle produced by the loss or gain of electrons.

Ion-exchange column A water softener which works by replacing calcium and magnesium ions with sodium or hydrogen ions, removing the hardness.

Ionic bonding The electrostatic force of attraction between positively and negatively charged ions.

Isotope Atom that has the same number of protons but different number of neutrons, i.e. it has the same atomic number but different mass number.

L

Limewater The common name for calcium hydroxide solution.

M

Macromolecule Giant covalent structure.

Mantle The layer of the Earth between its crust and its core.

Mass number The number of protons plus neutrons in the nucleus of an atom.

Mass spectrometer A machine that can be used to analyse small amounts of a substance to identify it and to find its relative molecular mass.

Mixture When some elements or compounds are mixed together and intermingle but do not react together (i.e. no new substance is made). A mixture is *not* a pure substance.

Mole The amount of substance in the relative atomic or formula mass of a substance in grams.

Molecular formula The chemical formula that shows the actual numbers of atoms in a particular molecule (e.g. C_2H_4).

Molecular ion peak The peak on the mass spectrum of a substance which tells us the relative molecular mass of the substance. The peak is produced by the heaviest positive ion shown on the mass spectrum.

Monomers Small reactive molecules that react together in repeating sequences to form a very large molecule (a polymer).

Mortar A building material used to bind bricks together. It is made by mixing cement and sand with water.

N

Nanoscience The study of very tiny particles or structures between 1 and 100 nanometres in size – where 1 nanometre = 10.9 metres.

Neutral A solution with a pH value of 7 that is neither acidic nor an alkaline. Alternatively, something that carries no overall electrical charge – neither positively nor negatively charged.

Neutralisation The chemical reaction of an acid with a base in which they cancel each other out, forming a salt and water. If the base is a carbonate or hydrogen carbonate, carbon dioxide is also produced in the reaction.

Neutron A dense particle found in the nucleus of an atom. It is electrically neutral, carrying no charge.

Nitrogen oxides Gaseous pollutants given off from motor vehicles, a cause of acid rain.

Nucleus The very small and dense central part of an atom which contains protons and neutrons.

O

Ore Rock which contains enough metal to make it economically worthwhile to extract the metal.

Oxidation The reaction when oxygen is added to a substance (or when electrons are lost).

Oxidised A reaction where oxygen is added to a substance (or when electrons are lost from a substance).

P

Particulate Small solid particle given off from motor vehicles as a result of incomplete combustion of its fuel.

Percentage yield The actual mass of product collected in a reaction divided by the maximum mass that could have been formed in theory, multiplied by 100.

Periodic table An arrangement of elements in the order of their atomic numbers, forming groups and periods.

Permanent hard water Hard water whose calcium and/or magnesium ions are not removed when the water is boiled, thus remaining hard.

pH scale A number that shows how strongly acidic or alkaline a solution is. Acids have a pH value of less than 7 (pH 1 is strongly acidic). Alkalis have a pH value above 7 (pH 14 is strongly alkaline). A neutral liquid has a pH value of 7.

Phytomining The process of extraction of metals from ores using plants.

Pipette A glass tube used to measure accurate volumes of liquids.

Polymer A substance made from very large molecules made up of many repeating units, for example, poly(ethene).

Polymerisation The reaction of monomers to make a polymer.

Precipitate An insoluble solid formed by a reaction taking place in solution.

Product A substance made as a result of a chemical reaction.

Propene An alkene with the formula C_3H_6.

Proton A tiny positive particle found inside the nucleus of an atom.

R

Reactant A substance we start with before a chemical reaction takes place.

Reactivity series A list of elements in order of their reactivity. The most reactive element is put at the top of the list.

Reduction A reaction in which oxygen is removed (or electrons are gained).

Relative atomic mass, A_r The average mass of the atoms of an element compared with carbon-12 (which is given a mass of exactly 12). The average mass must take into account the proportions of the naturally occurring isotopes of the element.

Relative formula mass, M_r The total of the relative atomic masses, added up in the ratio shown in the chemical formula, of a substance.

Retention time The time it takes a component in a mixture to pass through the column during gas chromatography.

Reversible reaction A reaction in which the products can re-form the reactants.

S

Salt A salt is a compound formed when some or all of the hydrogen in an acid is replaced by a metal (or by an ammonium ion). For example, potassium nitrate, KNO_3 (from nitric acid).

Saturated hydrocarbon Describes a hydrocarbon that contains as many hydrogen atoms as possible in each molecule.

Scale (limescale) The insoluble substance formed when temporary hard water is boiled.

Scum The precipitate formed when soap reacts with calcium and/or magnesium ions in hard water.

Shape memory alloy Mixture of metals which respond to changes in temperature.

Shell (or energy level) An area in an atom, around its nucleus, where the electrons are found.

Smart polymer Polymers that change in response to changes in their environment.

Smelting Heating a metal ore in order to extract its metal.

Soapless detergent A cleaning agent that does not produce scum when used with hard water.

Soft water Water containing no dissolved calcium and/or magnesium salts, so it easily forms a lather with soap.

Stainless steel A chromium–nickel alloy of steel which does not rust.

State symbol The abbreviations used in balanced symbol equations to show if reactants and products are solid (s), liquid (l), gas (g) or dissolved in water (aq).

Steel An alloy of iron with small amounts of carbon or other metals, such as nickel and chromium, added.

Strong acids Acids that ionise completely in aqueous solutions.

Sulfur dioxide A toxic gas whose formula is SO_2. It causes acid rain.

T

Tectonic plates The huge slabs of rock that make up the Earth's crust and top part of its mantle.

Temporary hard water Hard water which is softened when it is boiled.

Thermal decomposition The breakdown of a compound by heat.

Thermosetting polymer Polymer that can form extensive cross-linking between chains, resulting in rigid materials which are heat-resistant.

Thermosoftening polymer Polymer that forms plastics which can be softened by heat, then remoulded into different shapes as they cool down and set.

Titanium A shiny, corrosion-resistant metal used to make alloys.

Titration A method for measuring the volumes of two solutions that react together.

Transition element Element from the central block of the periodic table. It has typical metallic properties and forms a coloured compound.

Transition metal See Transition element.

U

Universal indicator A mixture of indicators which can change through a range of colours depending on the pH of a solution. Its colour is matched to a pH number using a pH scale. It shows how strongly acidic or alkaline liquids and solutions are.

Unsaturated hydrocarbon A hydrocarbon whose molecules contain at least one carbon–carbon double bond.

Unsaturated oil Plant oil whose molecules contain at least one carbon–carbon double bond.

V

Vegetable oil Oil extracted from plants.

Viscosity The resistance of a liquid to flowing or the 'thickness' or resistance of a liquid to pouring.

W

Weak acids Acids that do not ionise completely in aqueous solutions.

Y

Yield See Percentage yield.